INJUSTICE

GODS AMONG US: YEAR FIVE

VOLUME 3

INJU
GODS AMON

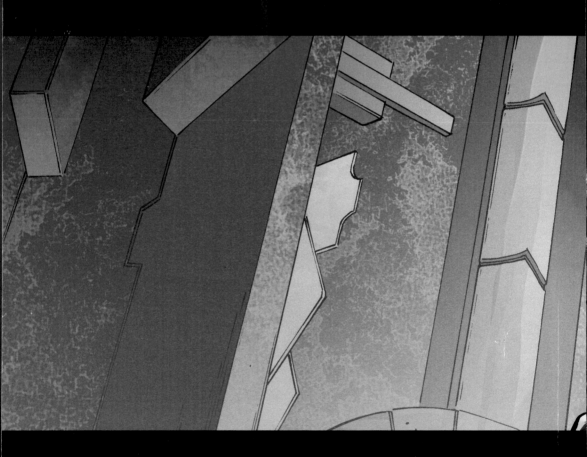

Brian Buccellato
Writer

Mike S. Miller Tom Derenick
Xermanico Marco Santucci
Artists

J. Nanjan Rex Lokus
Colorists

Wes Abbott
Letterer

David Yardin
Collection and series cover artist

STICE

US: YEAR FIVE

VOLUME 3

JIM CHADWICK · Editor – Original Series
DAVID PIÑA Assistant Editor – Original Series
JEB WOODARD Group Editor – Collected Editions
PAUL SANTOS Editor – Collected Edition
STEVE COOK Design Director – Books
AMIE BROCKWAY-METCALF Publication Design

BOB HARRAS Senior VP – Editor-in-Chief, DC Comics
PAT McCALLUM Executive Editor, DC Comics

DIANE NELSON President
DAN DiDIO Publisher
JIM LEE Publisher
GEOFF JOHNS President & Chief Creative Officer
AMIT DESAI Executive VP – Business & Marketing Strategy,
Direct to Consumer & Global Franchise Management
SAM ADES Senior VP & General Manager, Digital Services
BOBBIE CHASE VP & Executive Editor, Young Reader & Talent Development
MARK CHIARELLO Senior VP – Art, Design & Collected Editions
JOHN CUNNINGHAM Senior VP – Sales & Trade Marketing
ANNE DePIES Senior VP – Business Strategy, Finance & Administration
DON FALLETTI VP – Manufacturing Operations
LAWRENCE GANEM VP – Editorial Administration & Talent Relations
ALISON GILL Senior VP – Manufacturing & Operations
HANK KANALZ Senior VP – Editorial Strategy & Administration
JAY KOGAN VP – Legal Affairs
JACK MAHAN VP – Business Affairs
NICK J. NAPOLITANO VP – Manufacturing Administration
EDDIE SCANNELL VP – Consumer Marketing
COURTNEY SIMMONS Senior VP – Publicity & Communications
JIM (SKI) SOKOLOWSKI VP – Comic Book Specialty Sales & Trade Marketing
NANCY SPEARS VP – Mass, Book, Digital Sales & Trade Marketing
MICHELE R. WELLS VP - Content Strategy

INJUSTICE: GODS AMONG US – YEAR FIVE VOLUME 3

Published by DC Comics. Compilation and all new material
Copyright © 2017 DC Comics. All Rights Reserved. Originally
published in single magazine form in INJUSTICE: GODS
AMONG US YEAR FIVE 15-20.and INUSTICE: GODS AMONG
US YEAR FIVE ANNUAL 1 Copyright © 2016 DC Comics. All
Rights Reserved. All characters, their distinctive likenesses ar
related elements featured in this publication are trademarks
DC Comics. The stories, characters and incidents featured in
this publication are entirely fictional. DC Comics does not rea
or accept unsolicited submissions of ideas, stories or artwork

DC Comics, 2900 West Alameda Ave., Burbank, CA 91505
Printed by LSC Communications, Kendallville, IN, USA. 9/8/17
First Printing. ISBN: 978-1-4012-7426-9

Library of Congress Cataloging-in-Publication Data is availab

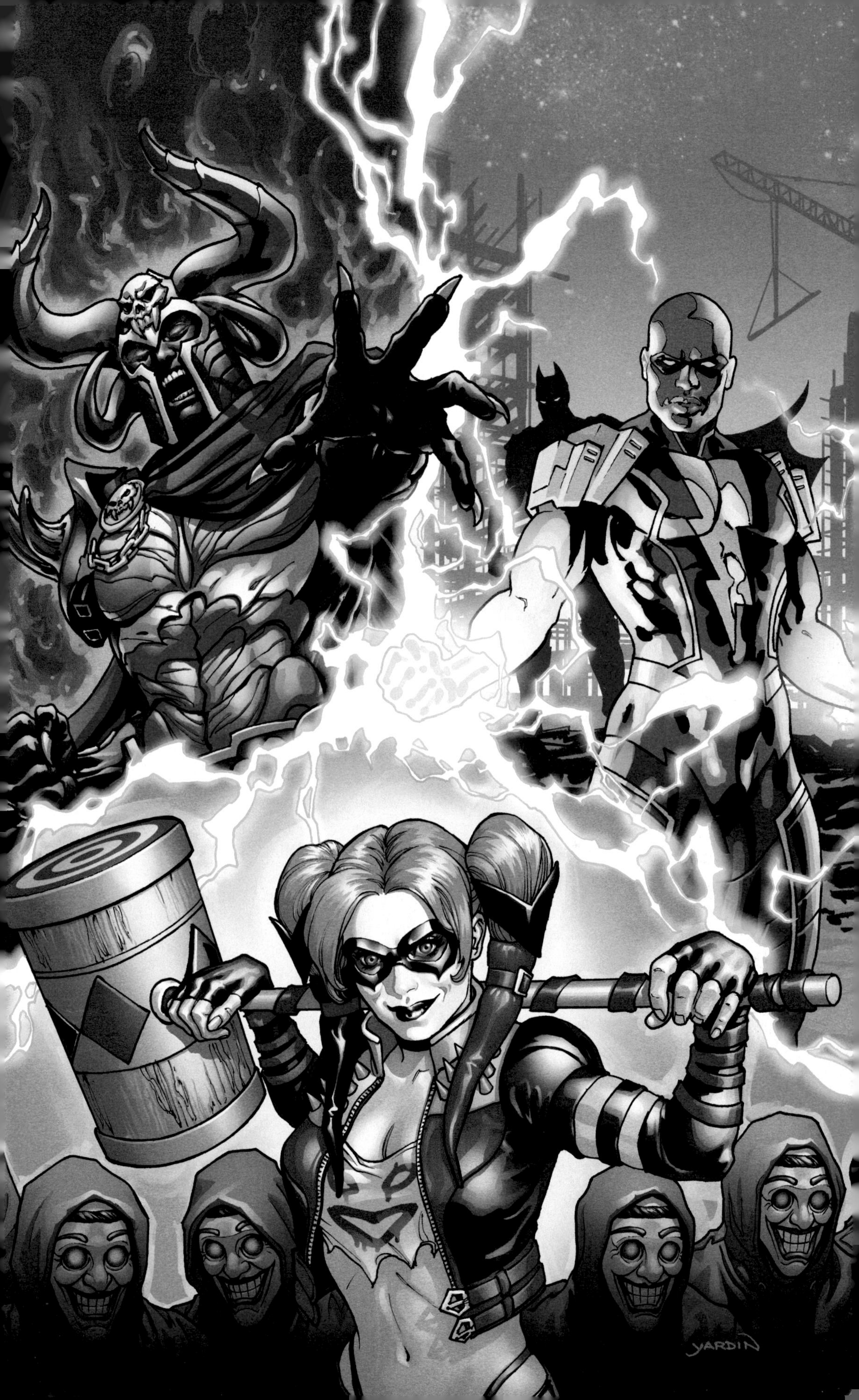
YARDIN

"The Clan" **Mike S. Miller** Artist **J. Nanjan** Colorist
"Ares" **Xermanico** Artist **Rex Lokus** Colorist
"Reconstruction" **Marco Santucci** Artist **Rex Lokus** Colorist

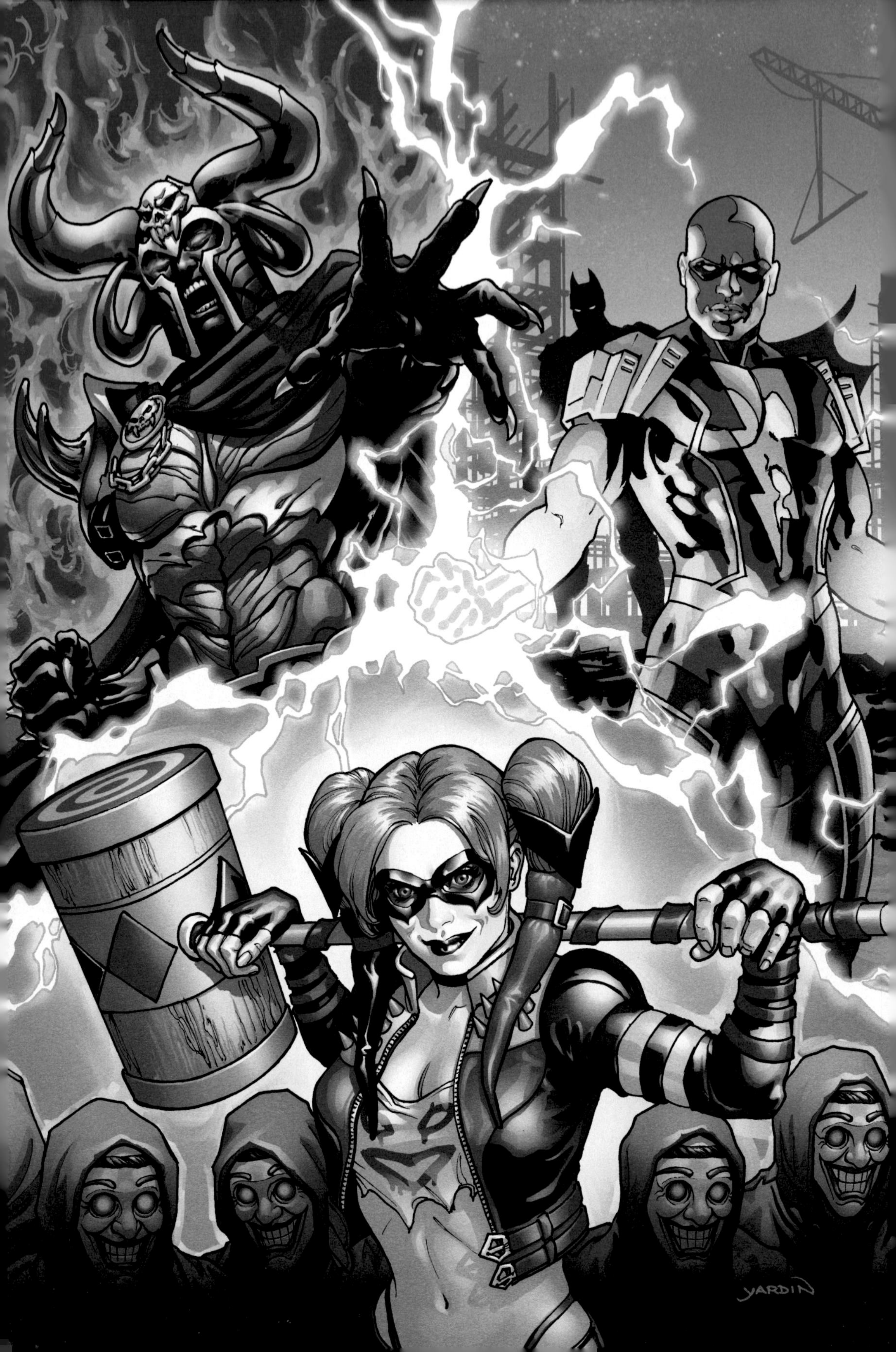
YARDIN

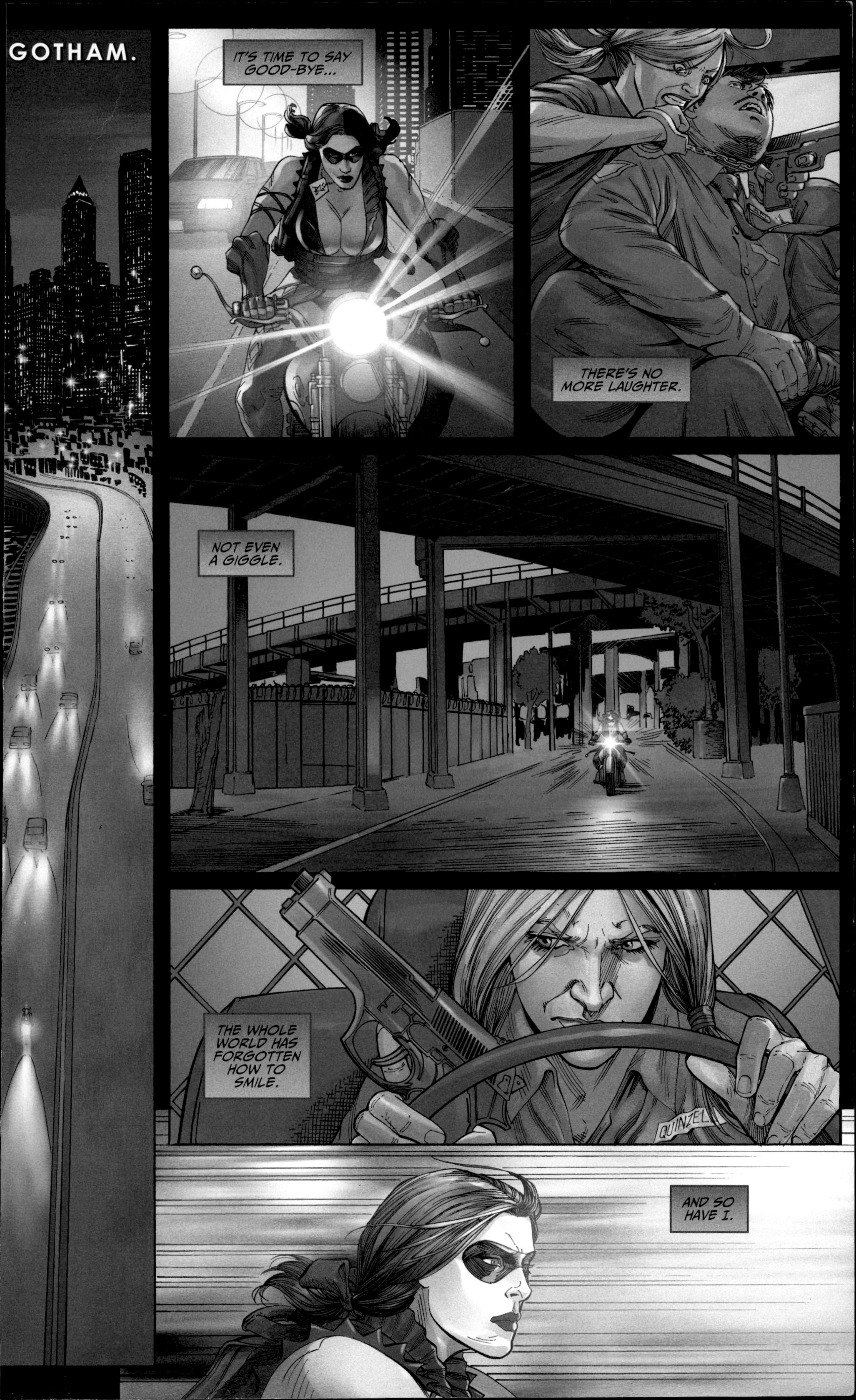
GOTHAM.
IT'S TIME TO SAY GOOD-BYE...
THERE'S NO MORE LAUGHTER.
NOT EVEN A GIGGLE.
THE WHOLE WORLD HAS FORGOTTEN HOW TO SMILE.
QUINZEL
AND SO HAVE I.

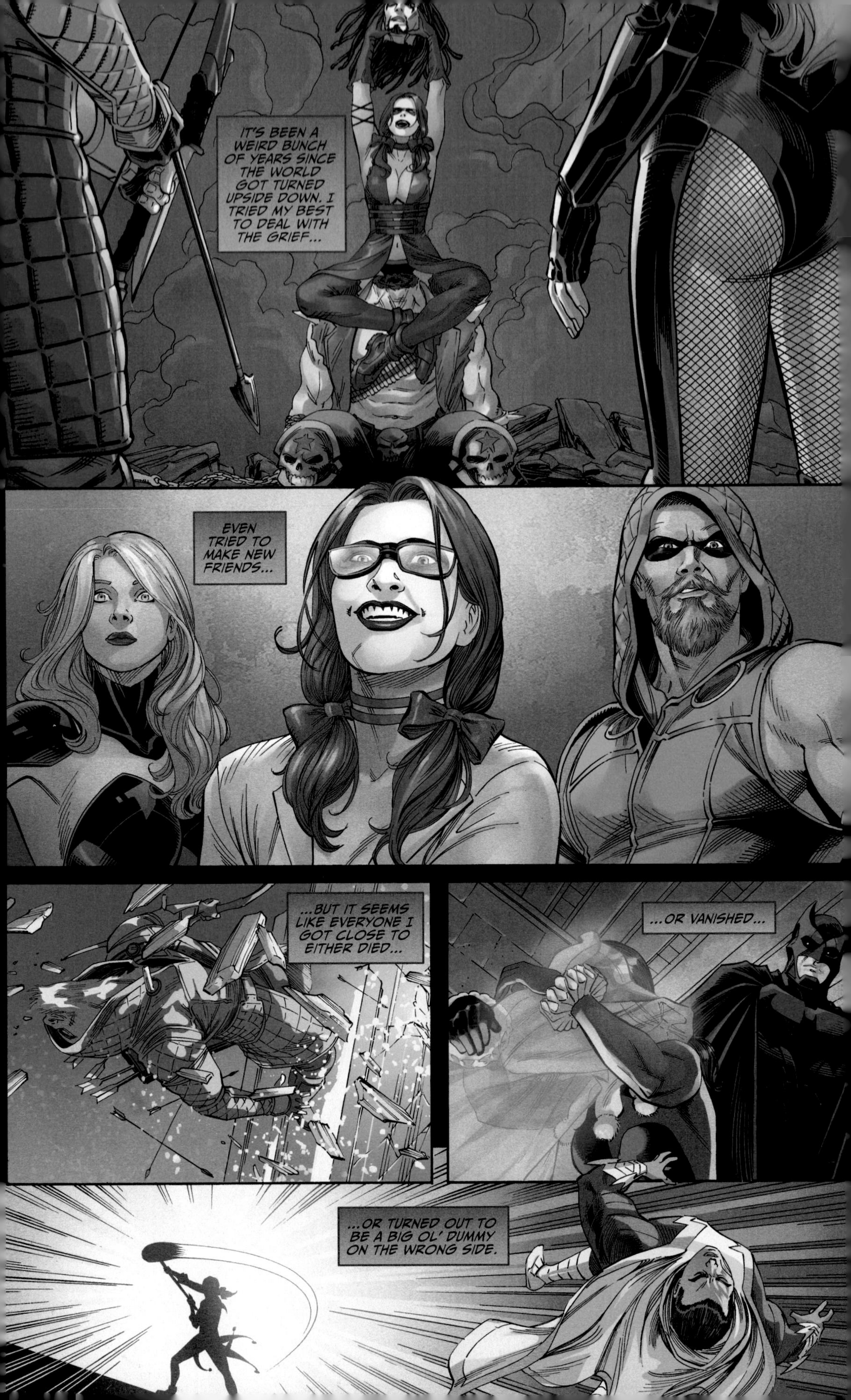
IT'S BEEN A WEIRD BUNCH OF YEARS SINCE THE WORLD GOT TURNED UPSIDE DOWN. I TRIED MY BEST TO DEAL WITH THE GRIEF...
EVEN TRIED TO MAKE NEW FRIENDS...
...BUT IT SEEMS LIKE EVERYONE I GOT CLOSE TO EITHER DIED...
...OR VANISHED...
...OR TURNED OUT TO BE A BIG OL' DUMMY ON THE WRONG SIDE.

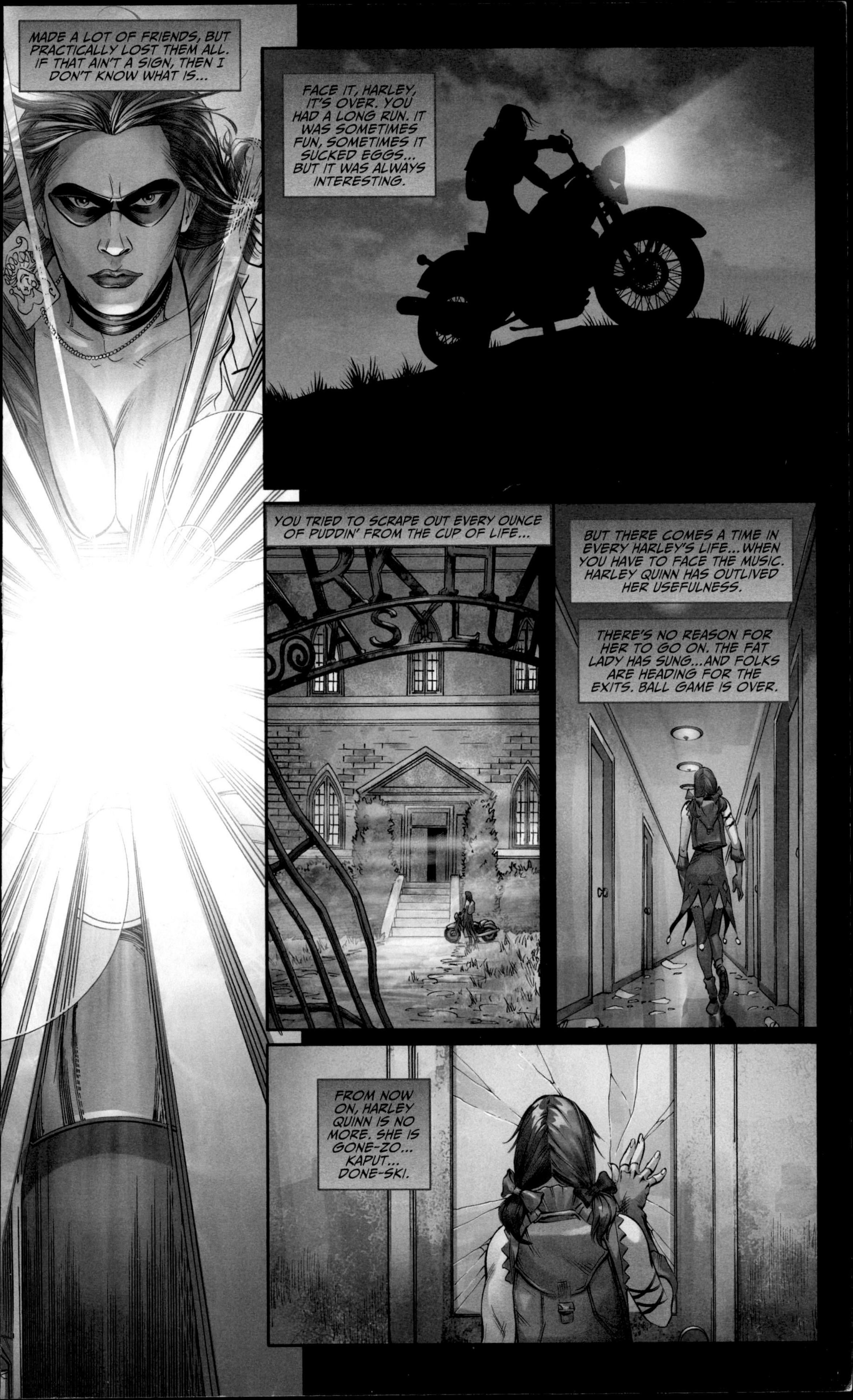
MADE A LOT OF FRIENDS, BUT PRACTICALLY LOST THEM ALL. IF THAT AIN'T A SIGN, THEN I DON'T KNOW WHAT IS...
FACE IT, HARLEY, IT'S OVER. YOU HAD A LONG RUN. IT WAS SOMETIMES FUN, SOMETIMES IT SUCKED EGGS... BUT IT WAS ALWAYS INTERESTING.
YOU TRIED TO SCRAPE OUT EVERY OUNCE OF PUDDIN' FROM THE CUP OF LIFE...
BUT THERE COMES A TIME IN EVERY HARLEY'S LIFE... WHEN YOU HAVE TO FACE THE MUSIC. HARLEY QUINN HAS OUTLIVED HER USEFULNESS.
THERE'S NO REASON FOR HER TO GO ON. THE FAT LADY HAS SUNG... AND FOLKS ARE HEADING FOR THE EXITS. BALL GAME IS OVER.
FROM NOW ON, HARLEY QUINN IS NO MORE. SHE IS GONE-ZO... KAPUT... DONE-SKI.

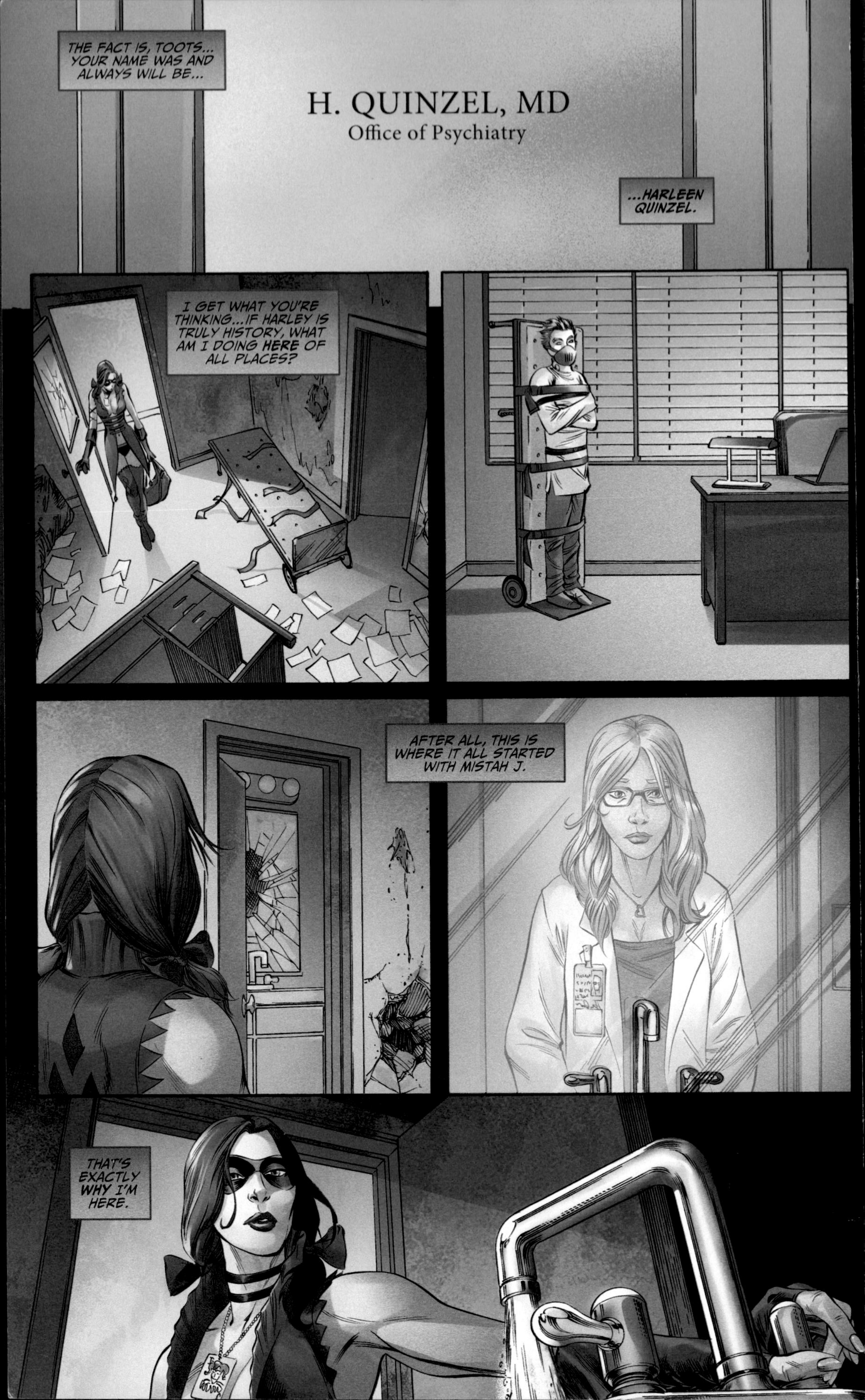
THE FACT IS, TOOTS... YOUR NAME WAS AND ALWAYS WILL BE...
H. QUINZEL, MD
Office of Psychiatry
...HARLEEN QUINZEL.
I GET WHAT YOU'RE THINKING...IF HARLEY IS TRULY HISTORY, WHAT AM I DOING HERE OF ALL PLACES?
AFTER ALL, THIS IS WHERE IT ALL STARTED WITH MISTAH J.
THAT'S EXACTLY WHY I'M HERE.

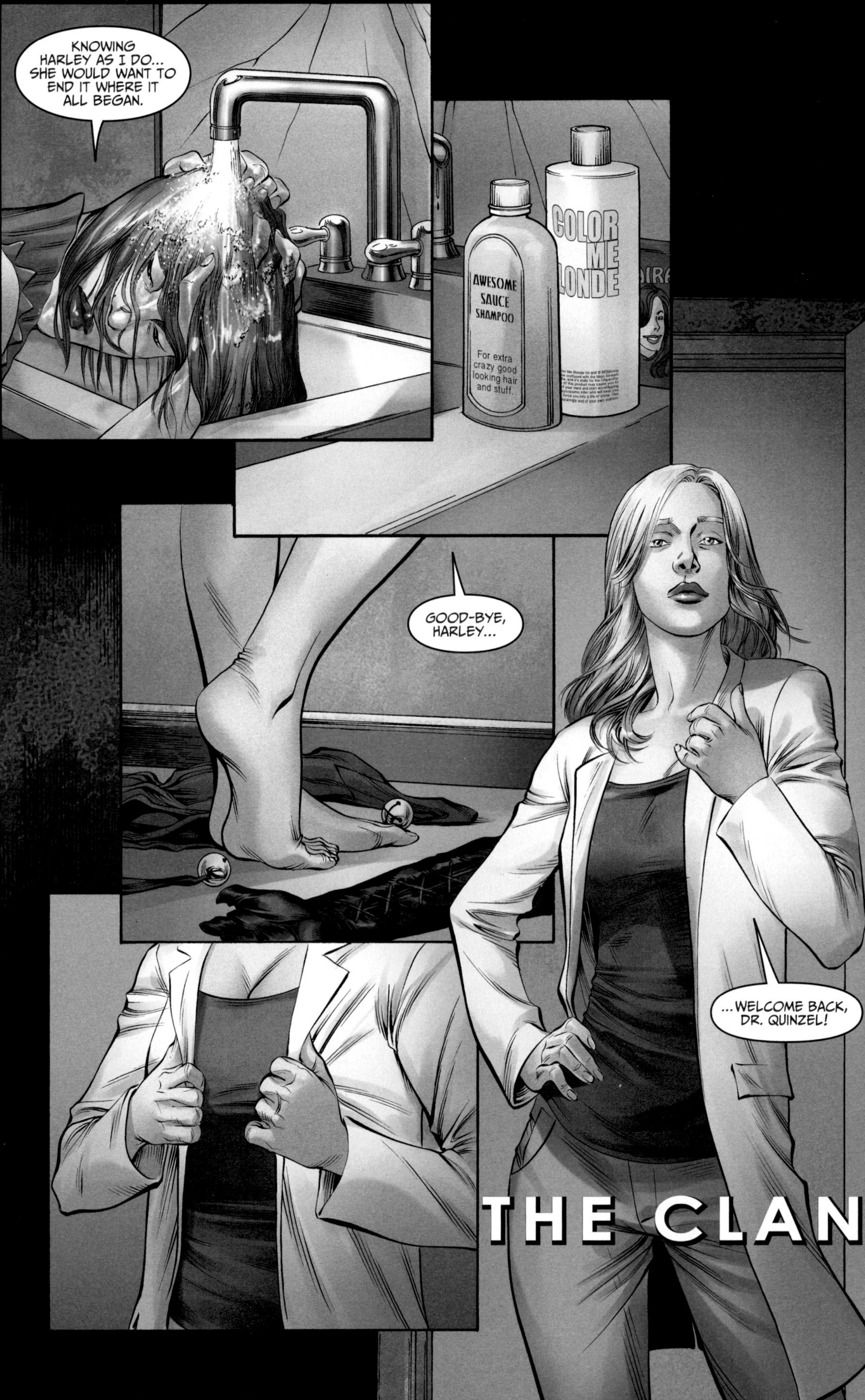
KNOWING HARLEY AS I DO... SHE WOULD WANT TO END IT WHERE IT ALL BEGAN.
AWESOME SAUCE SHAMPOO
For extra crazy good looking hair and stuff.
COLOR ME
LONDE
GOOD-BYE, HARLEY...
...WELCOME BACK, DR. QUINZEL!
THE CLAN

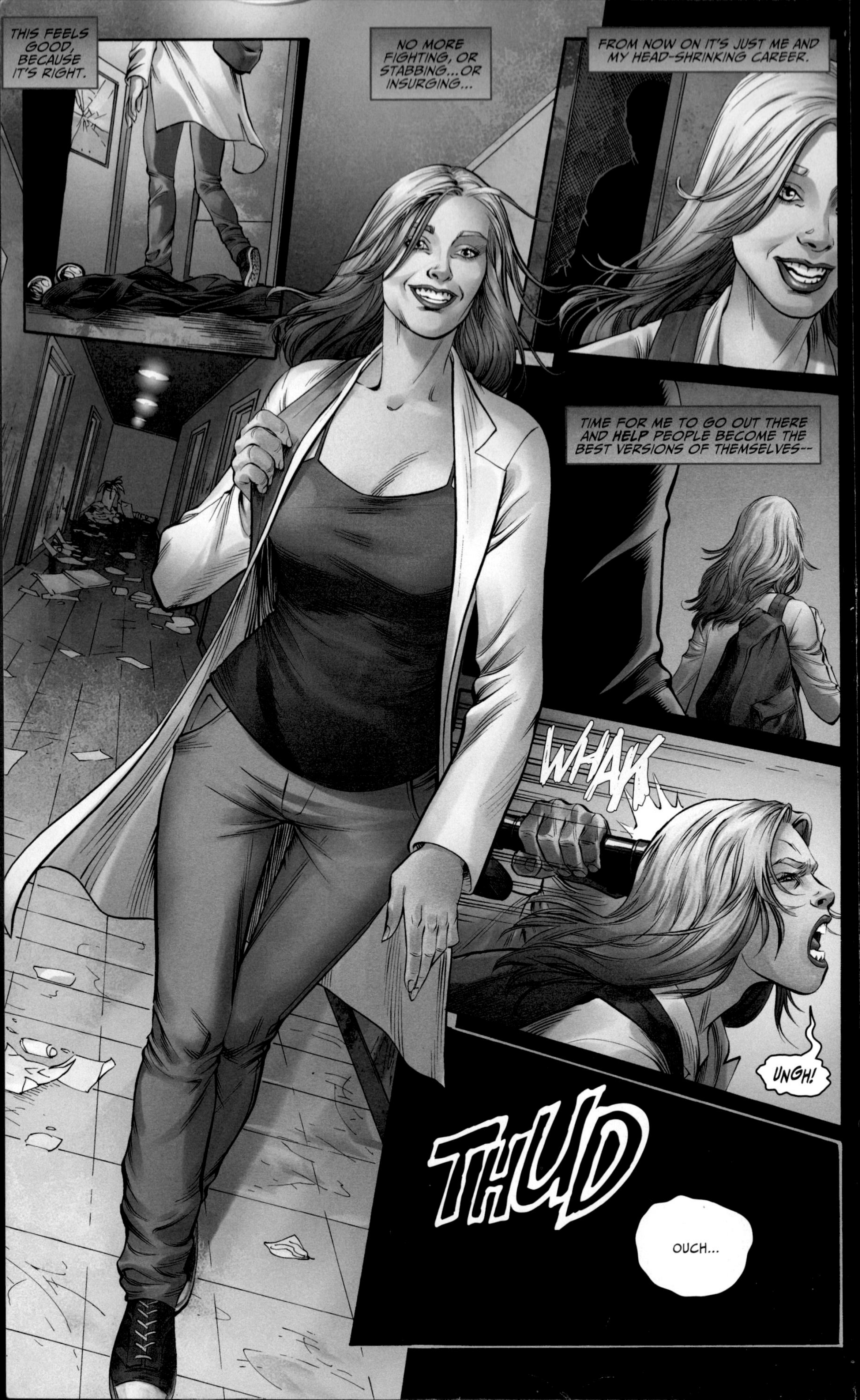
THIS FEELS GOOD, BECAUSE IT'S RIGHT.
NO MORE FIGHTING, OR STABBING...OR INSURGING...
FROM NOW ON IT'S JUST ME AND MY HEAD-SHRINKING CAREER.
TIME FOR ME TO GO OUT THERE AND **HELP** PEOPLE BECOME THE BEST VERSIONS OF THEMSELVES--
WHAK
UNGH!
THUD
OUCH...

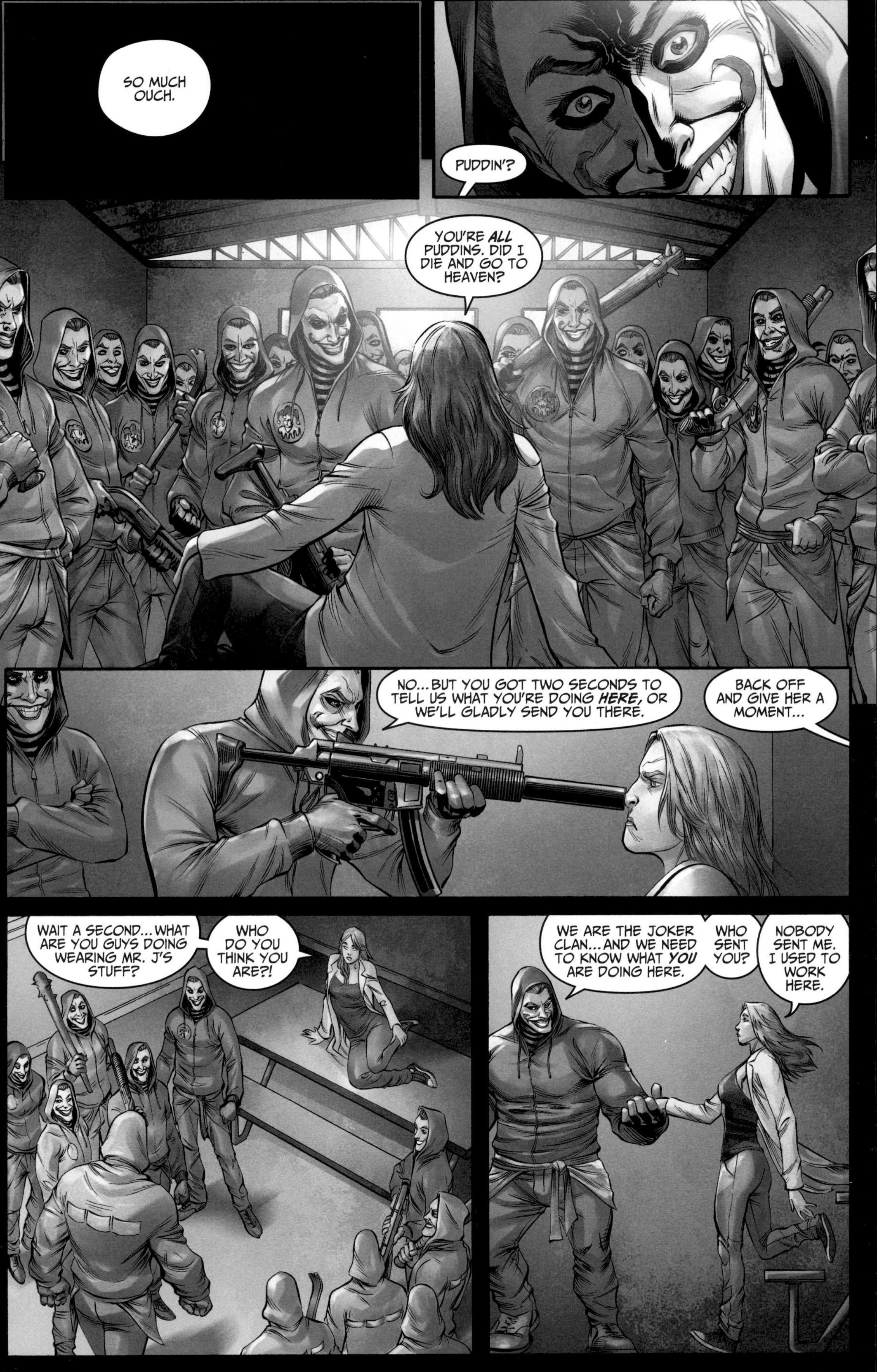

SO MUCH OUCH.
PUDDIN'?
YOU'RE *ALL* PUDDINS. DID I DIE AND GO TO HEAVEN?
NO... BUT YOU GOT TWO SECONDS TO TELL US WHAT YOU'RE DOING *HERE,* OR WE'LL GLADLY SEND YOU THERE.
BACK OFF AND GIVE HER A MOMENT...
WAIT A SECOND... WHAT ARE YOU GUYS DOING WEARING MR. J'S STUFF?
WHO DO YOU THINK YOU ARE?!
WE ARE THE JOKER CLAN... AND WE NEED TO KNOW WHAT *YOU* ARE DOING HERE.
WHO SENT YOU?
NOBODY SENT ME. I USED TO WORK HERE.

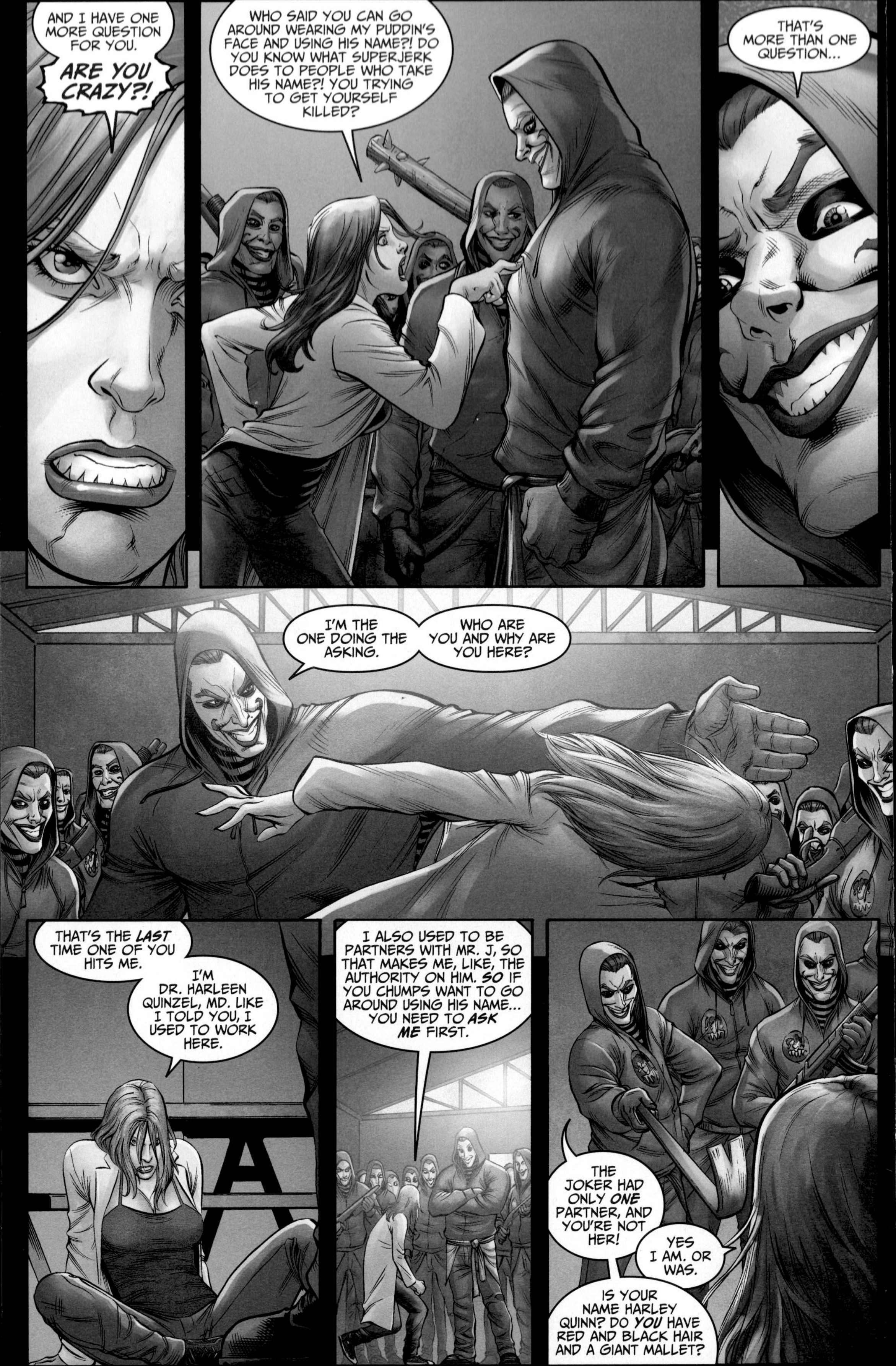
AND I HAVE ONE MORE QUESTION FOR YOU.
ARE YOU CRAZY?!
WHO SAID YOU CAN GO AROUND WEARING MY PUDDIN'S FACE AND USING HIS NAME?! DO YOU KNOW WHAT SUPERJERK DOES TO PEOPLE WHO TAKE HIS NAME?! YOU TRYING TO GET YOURSELF KILLED?
THAT'S MORE THAN ONE QUESTION...
I'M THE ONE DOING THE ASKING.
WHO ARE YOU AND WHY ARE YOU HERE?
THAT'S THE LAST TIME ONE OF YOU HITS ME.
I'M DR. HARLEEN QUINZEL, MD. LIKE I TOLD YOU, I USED TO WORK HERE.
I ALSO USED TO BE PARTNERS WITH MR. J, SO THAT MAKES ME, LIKE, THE AUTHORITY ON HIM. SO IF YOU CHUMPS WANT TO GO AROUND USING HIS NAME... YOU NEED TO ASK ME FIRST.
THE JOKER HAD ONLY ONE PARTNER, AND YOU'RE NOT HER!
YES I AM. OR WAS.
IS YOUR NAME HARLEY QUINN? DO YOU HAVE RED AND BLACK HAIR AND A GIANT MALLET?

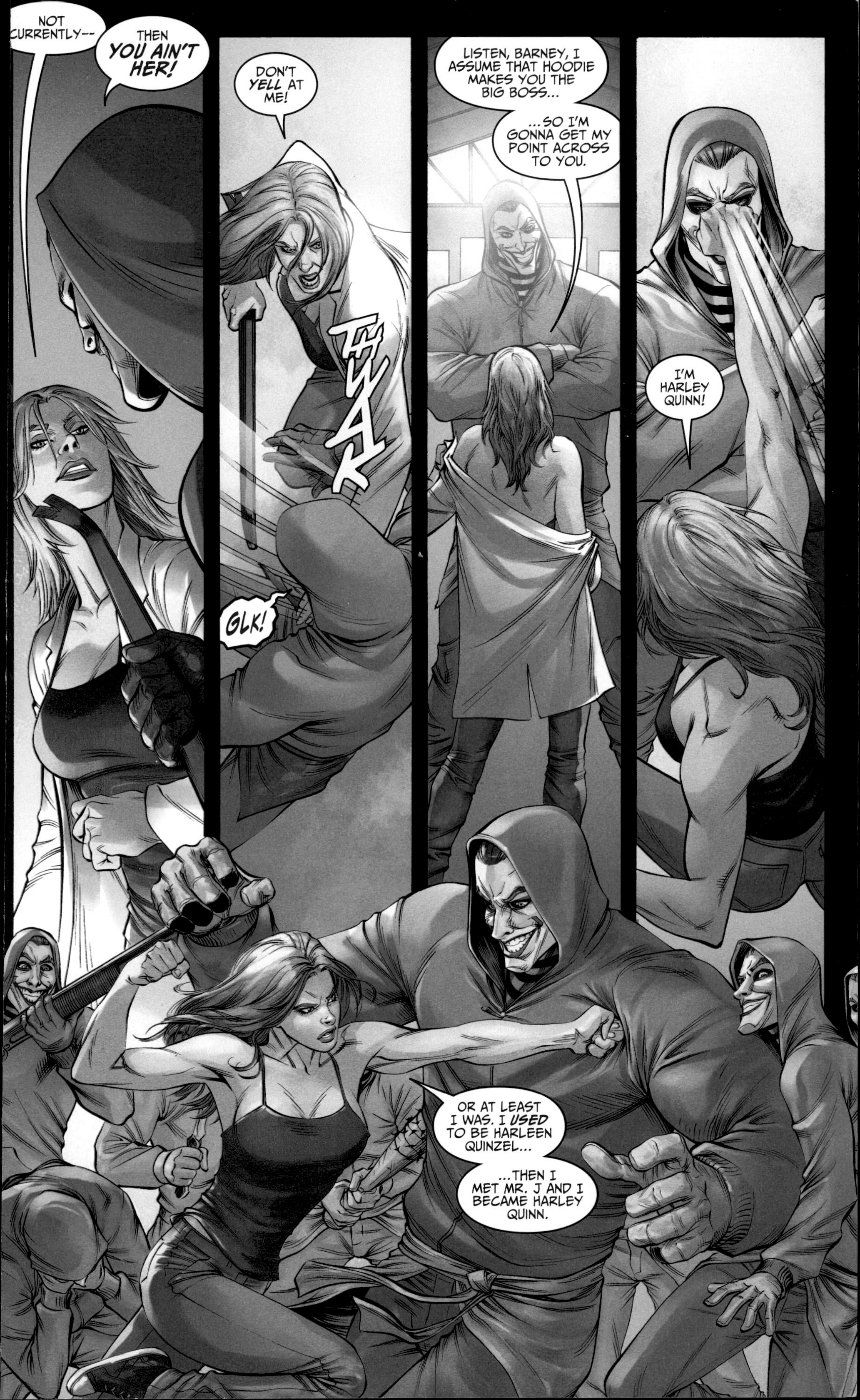
NOT CURRENTLY--
THEN YOU AIN'T HER!
DON'T YELL AT ME!
THWAK
GLK!
LISTEN, BARNEY, I ASSUME THAT HOODIE MAKES YOU THE BIG BOSS...
...SO I'M GONNA GET MY POINT ACROSS TO YOU.
I'M HARLEY QUINN!
OR AT LEAST I WAS. I USED TO BE HARLEEN QUINZEL...
...THEN I MET MR. J AND I BECAME HARLEY QUINN.

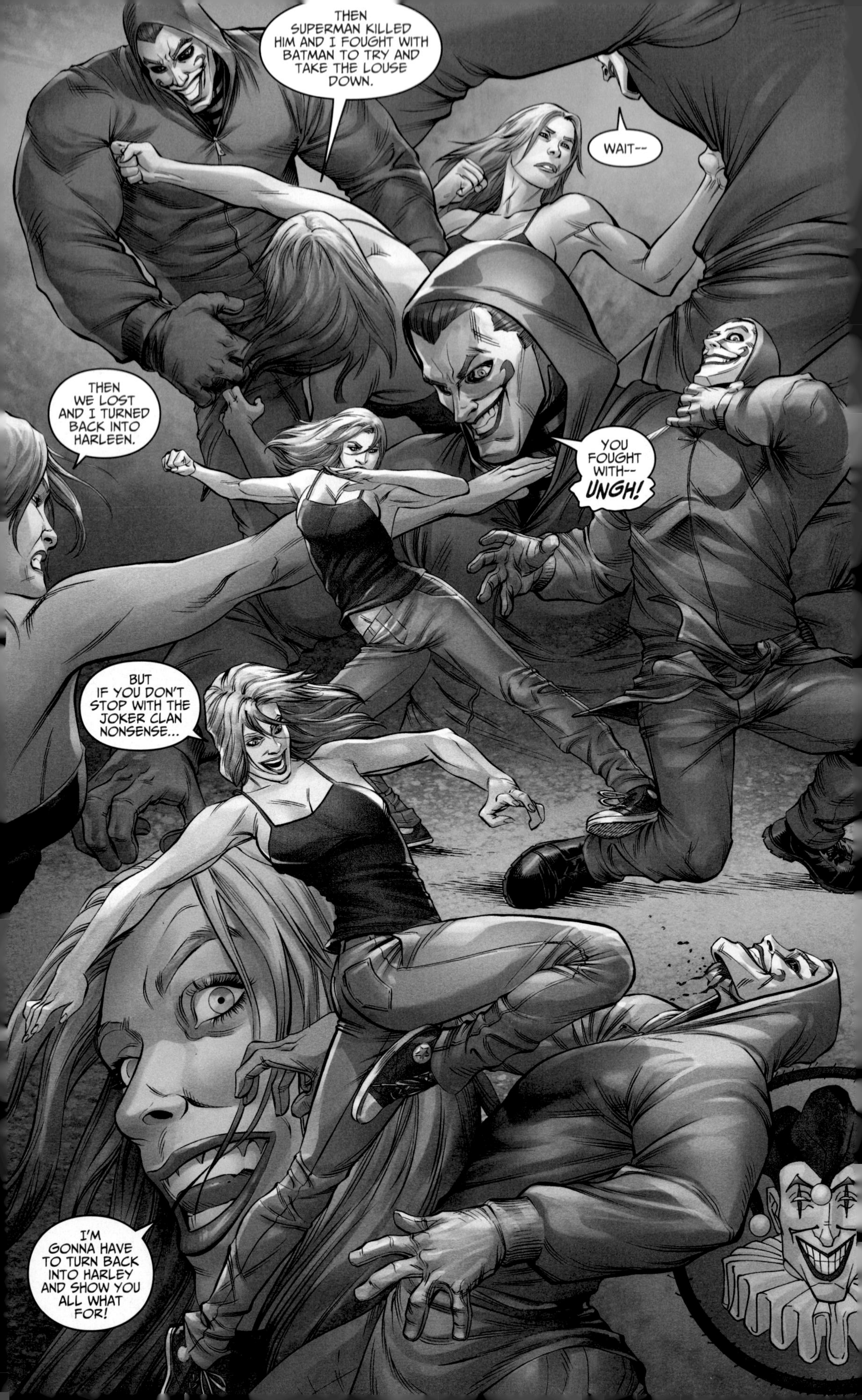
THEN SUPERMAN KILLED HIM AND I FOUGHT WITH BATMAN TO TRY AND TAKE THE LOUSE DOWN.
WAIT--
THEN WE LOST AND I TURNED BACK INTO HARLEEN.
YOU FOUGHT WITH-- UNGH!
BUT IF YOU DON'T STOP WITH THE JOKER CLAN NONSENSE...
I'M GONNA HAVE TO TURN BACK INTO HARLEY AND SHOW YOU ALL WHAT FOR!

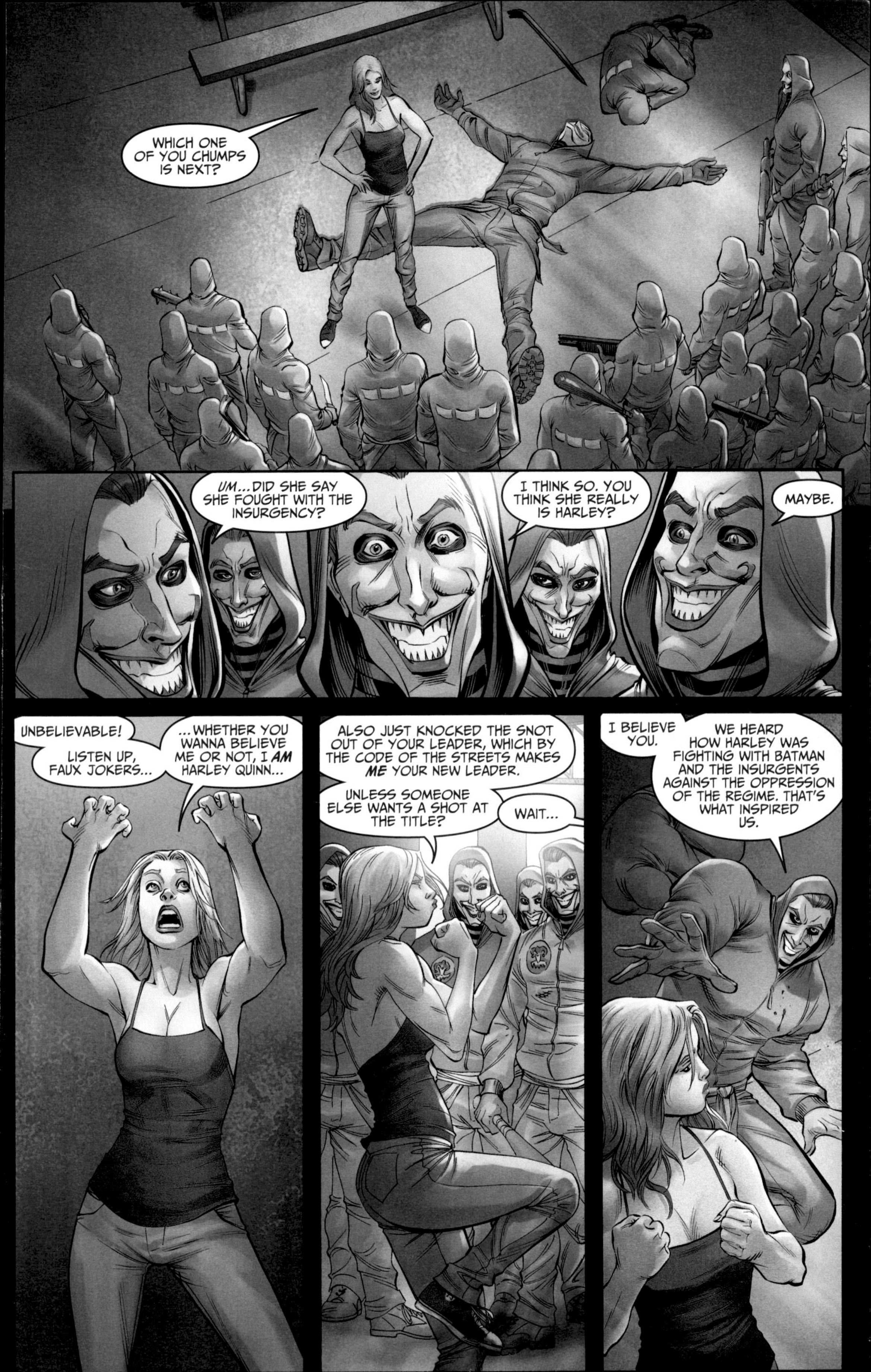
WHICH ONE OF YOU CHUMPS IS NEXT?
UM...DID SHE SAY SHE FOUGHT WITH THE INSURGENCY?
I THINK SO. YOU THINK SHE REALLY IS HARLEY?
MAYBE.
UNBELIEVABLE!
LISTEN UP, FAUX JOKERS...
...WHETHER YOU WANNA BELIEVE ME OR NOT, I AM HARLEY QUINN...
ALSO JUST KNOCKED THE SNOT OUT OF YOUR LEADER, WHICH BY THE CODE OF THE STREETS MAKES ME YOUR NEW LEADER.
UNLESS SOMEONE ELSE WANTS A SHOT AT THE TITLE?
WAIT...
I BELIEVE YOU.
WE HEARD HOW HARLEY WAS FIGHTING WITH BATMAN AND THE INSURGENTS AGAINST THE OPPRESSION OF THE REGIME. THAT'S WHAT INSPIRED US.

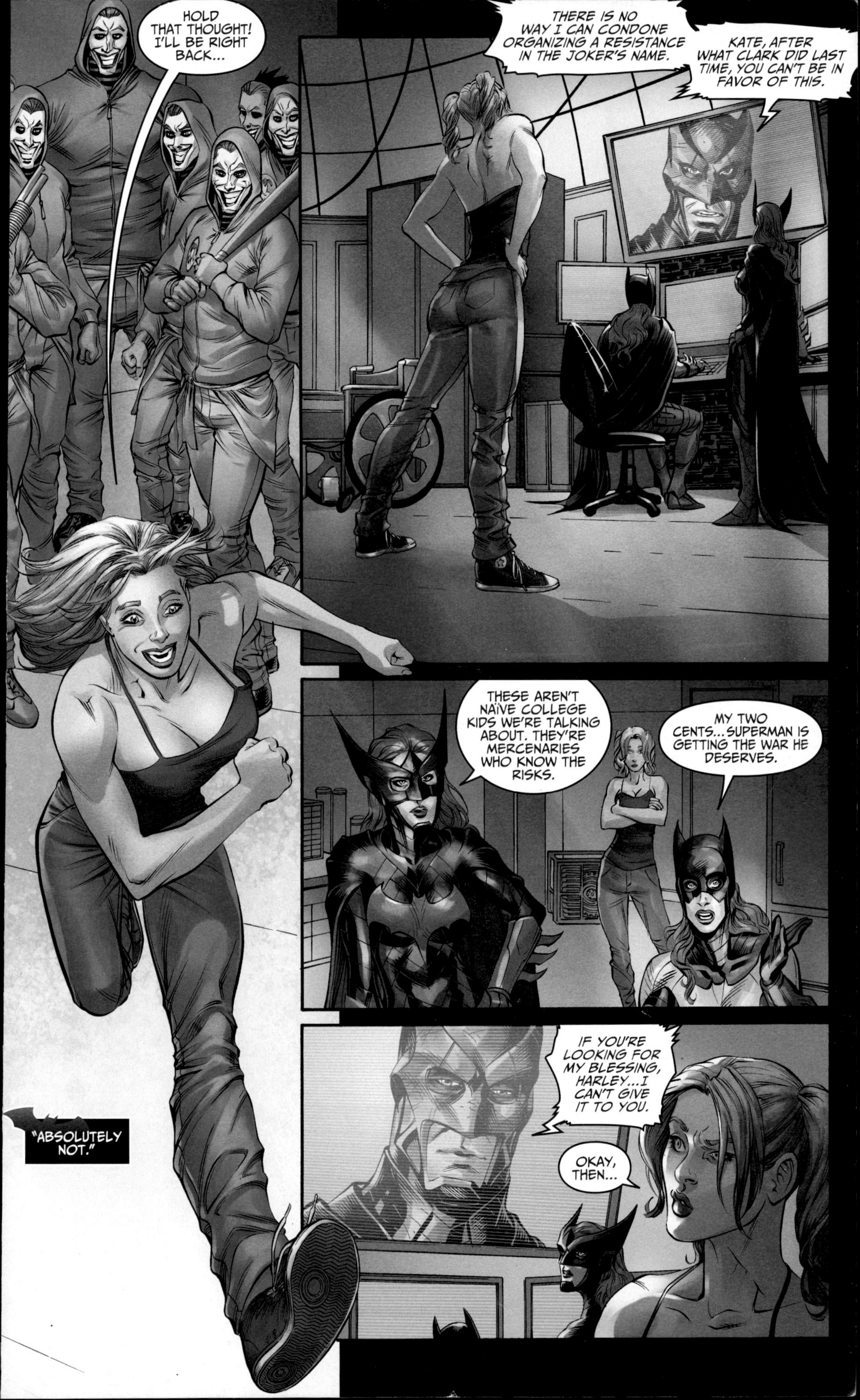
HOLD THAT THOUGHT! I'LL BE RIGHT BACK...
THERE IS NO WAY I CAN CONDONE ORGANIZING A RESISTANCE IN THE JOKER'S NAME.
KATE, AFTER WHAT CLARK DID LAST TIME, YOU CAN'T BE IN FAVOR OF THIS.
THESE AREN'T NAÏVE COLLEGE KIDS WE'RE TALKING ABOUT. THEY'RE MERCENARIES WHO KNOW THE RISKS.
MY TWO CENTS...SUPERMAN IS GETTING THE WAR HE DESERVES.
"ABSOLUTELY NOT."
IF YOU'RE LOOKING FOR MY BLESSING, HARLEY...I CAN'T GIVE IT TO YOU.
OKAY, THEN...

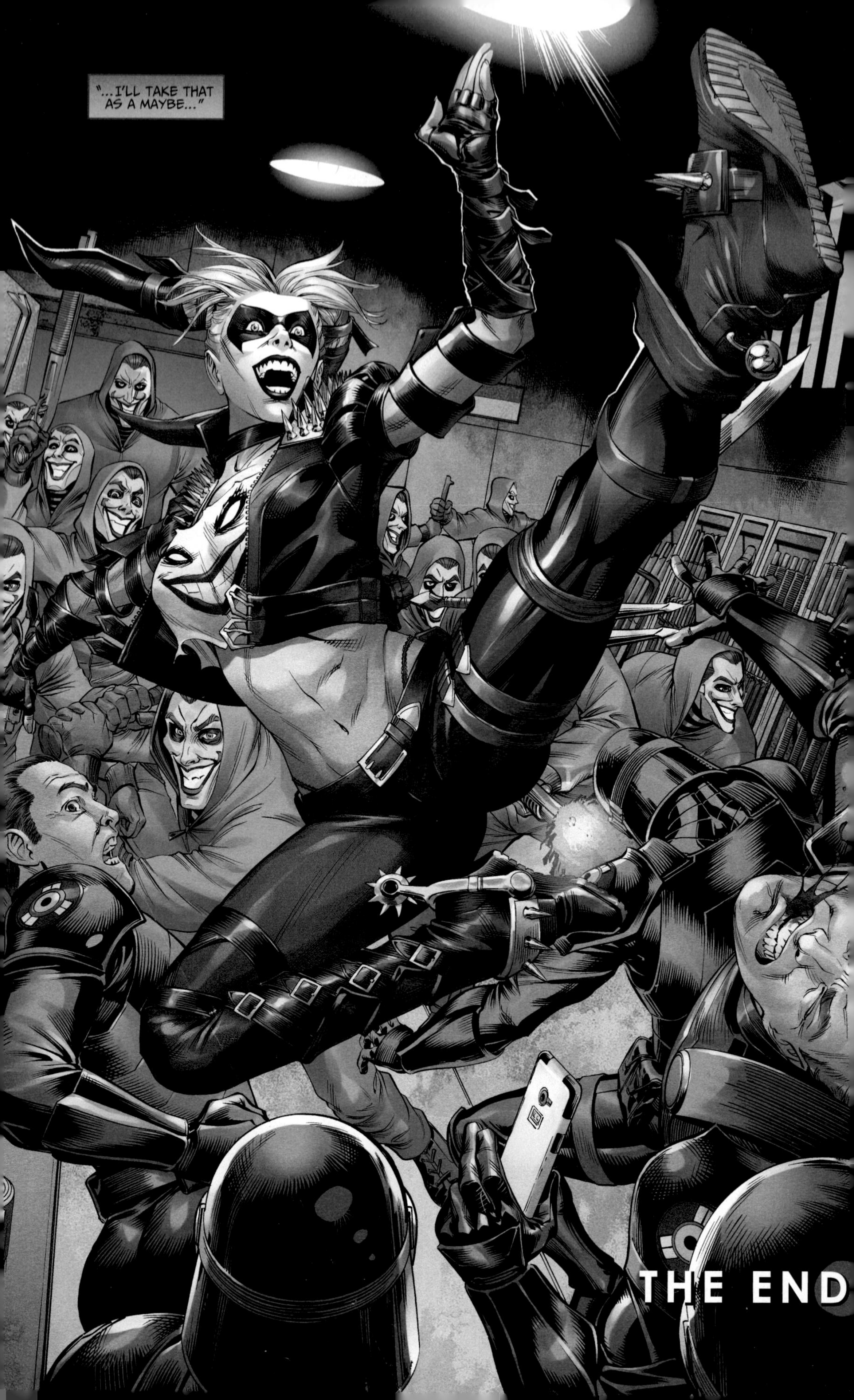
"...I'LL TAKE THAT AS A MAYBE..."
THE END

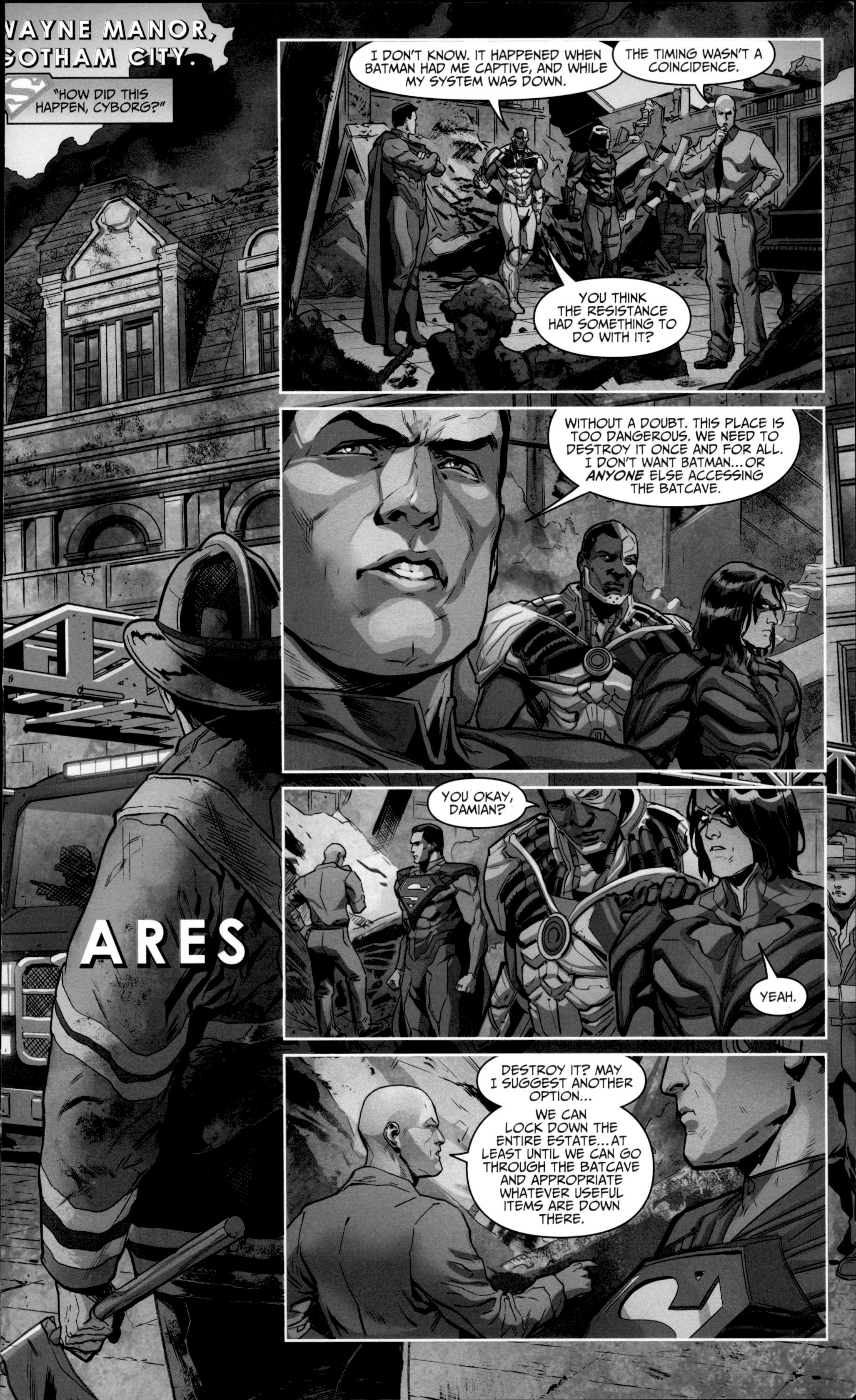
WAYNE MANOR, GOTHAM CITY.
"HOW DID THIS HAPPEN, CYBORG?"
I DON'T KNOW. IT HAPPENED WHEN BATMAN HAD ME CAPTIVE, AND WHILE MY SYSTEM WAS DOWN.
THE TIMING WASN'T A COINCIDENCE.
YOU THINK THE RESISTANCE HAD SOMETHING TO DO WITH IT?
WITHOUT A DOUBT. THIS PLACE IS TOO DANGEROUS. WE NEED TO DESTROY IT ONCE AND FOR ALL. I DON'T WANT BATMAN...OR *ANYONE* ELSE ACCESSING THE BATCAVE.
ARES
YOU OKAY, DAMIAN?
YEAH.
DESTROY IT? MAY I SUGGEST ANOTHER OPTION...
WE CAN LOCK DOWN THE ENTIRE ESTATE...AT LEAST UNTIL WE CAN GO THROUGH THE BATCAVE AND APPROPRIATE WHATEVER USEFUL ITEMS ARE DOWN THERE.

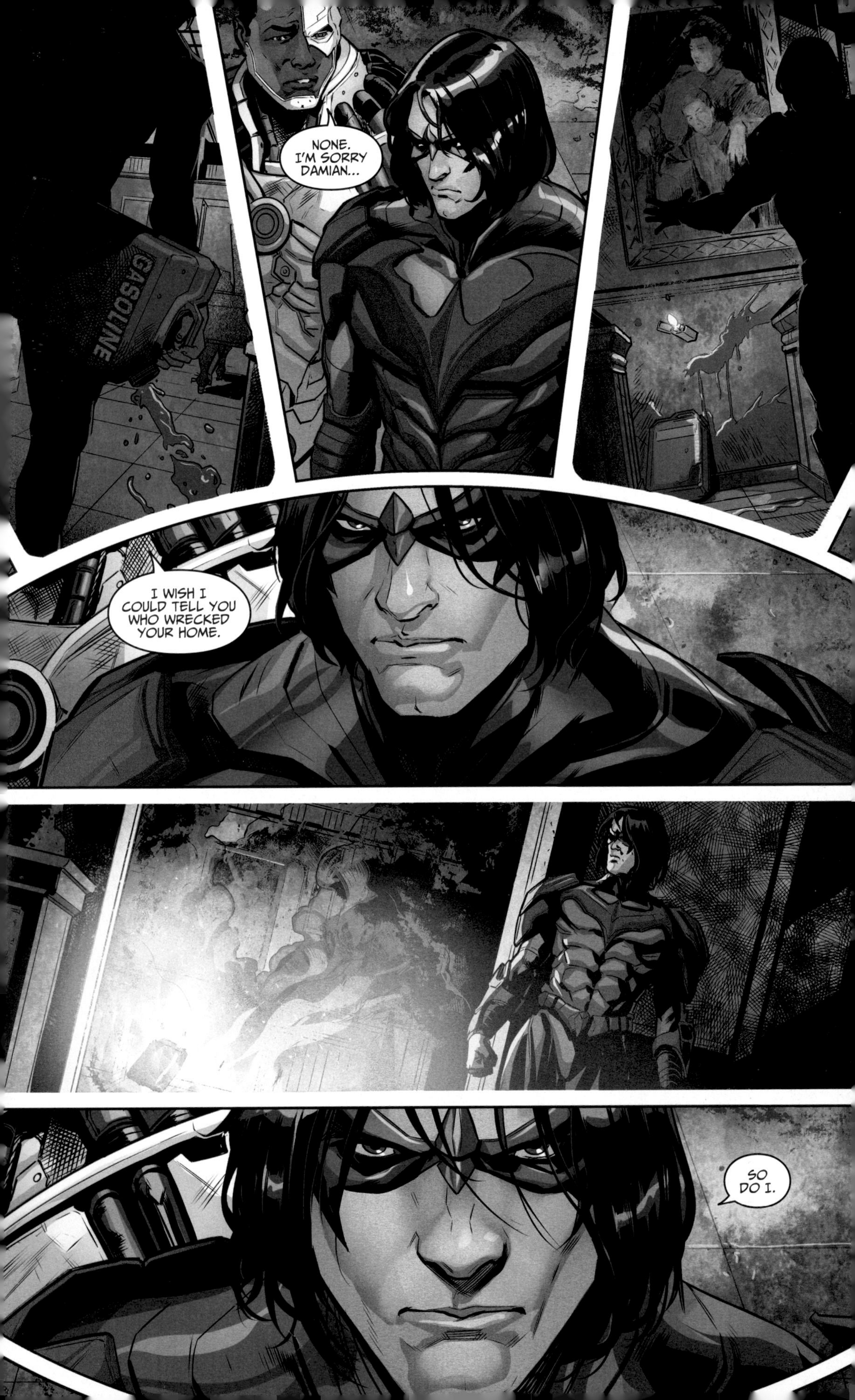
GASOLINE
NONE. I'M SORRY DAMIAN...
I WISH I COULD TELL YOU WHO WRECKED YOUR HOME.
SO DO I.

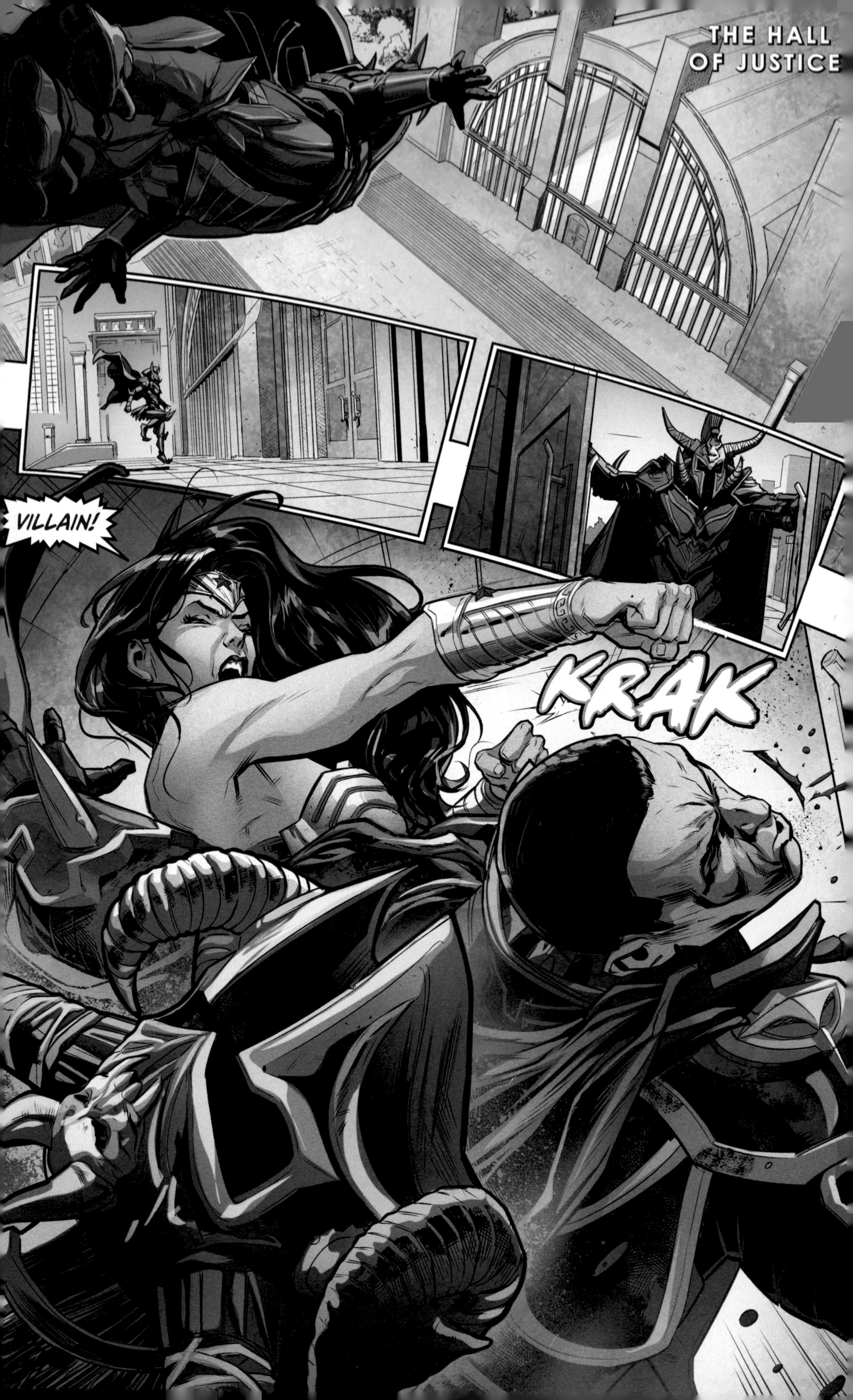
THE HALL
OF JUSTICE
VILLAIN!
KRAK

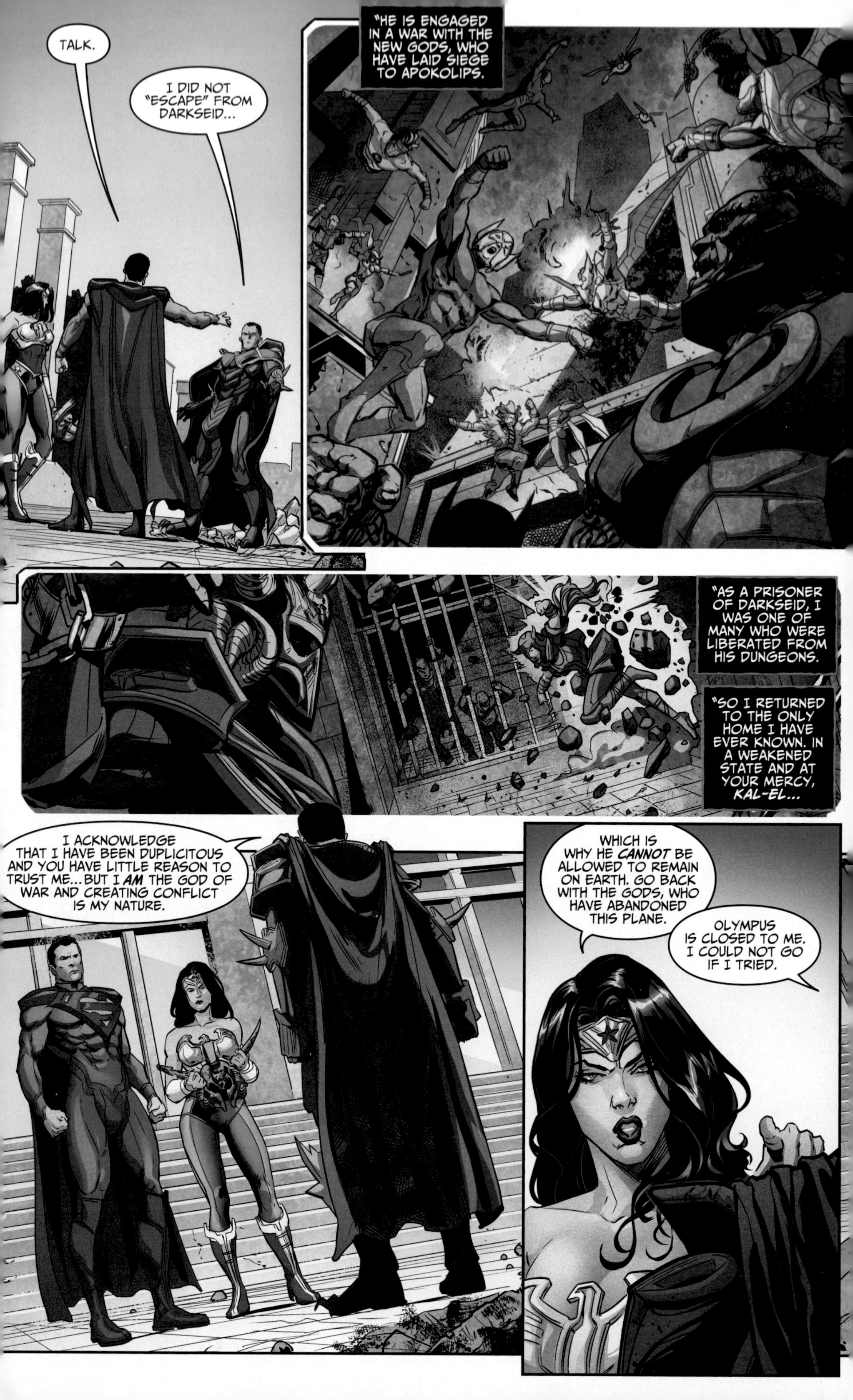
TALK.
I DID NOT "ESCAPE" FROM DARKSEID...
"HE IS ENGAGED IN A WAR WITH THE NEW GODS, WHO HAVE LAID SIEGE TO APOKOLIPS.
"AS A PRISONER OF DARKSEID, I WAS ONE OF MANY WHO WERE LIBERATED FROM HIS DUNGEONS.
"SO I RETURNED TO THE ONLY HOME I HAVE EVER KNOWN. IN A WEAKENED STATE AND AT YOUR MERCY, KAL-EL...
I ACKNOWLEDGE THAT I HAVE BEEN DUPLICITOUS AND YOU HAVE LITTLE REASON TO TRUST ME...BUT I AM THE GOD OF WAR AND CREATING CONFLICT IS MY NATURE.
WHICH IS WHY HE CANNOT BE ALLOWED TO REMAIN ON EARTH. GO BACK WITH THE GODS, WHO HAVE ABANDONED THIS PLANE.
OLYMPUS IS CLOSED TO ME. I COULD NOT GO IF I TRIED.

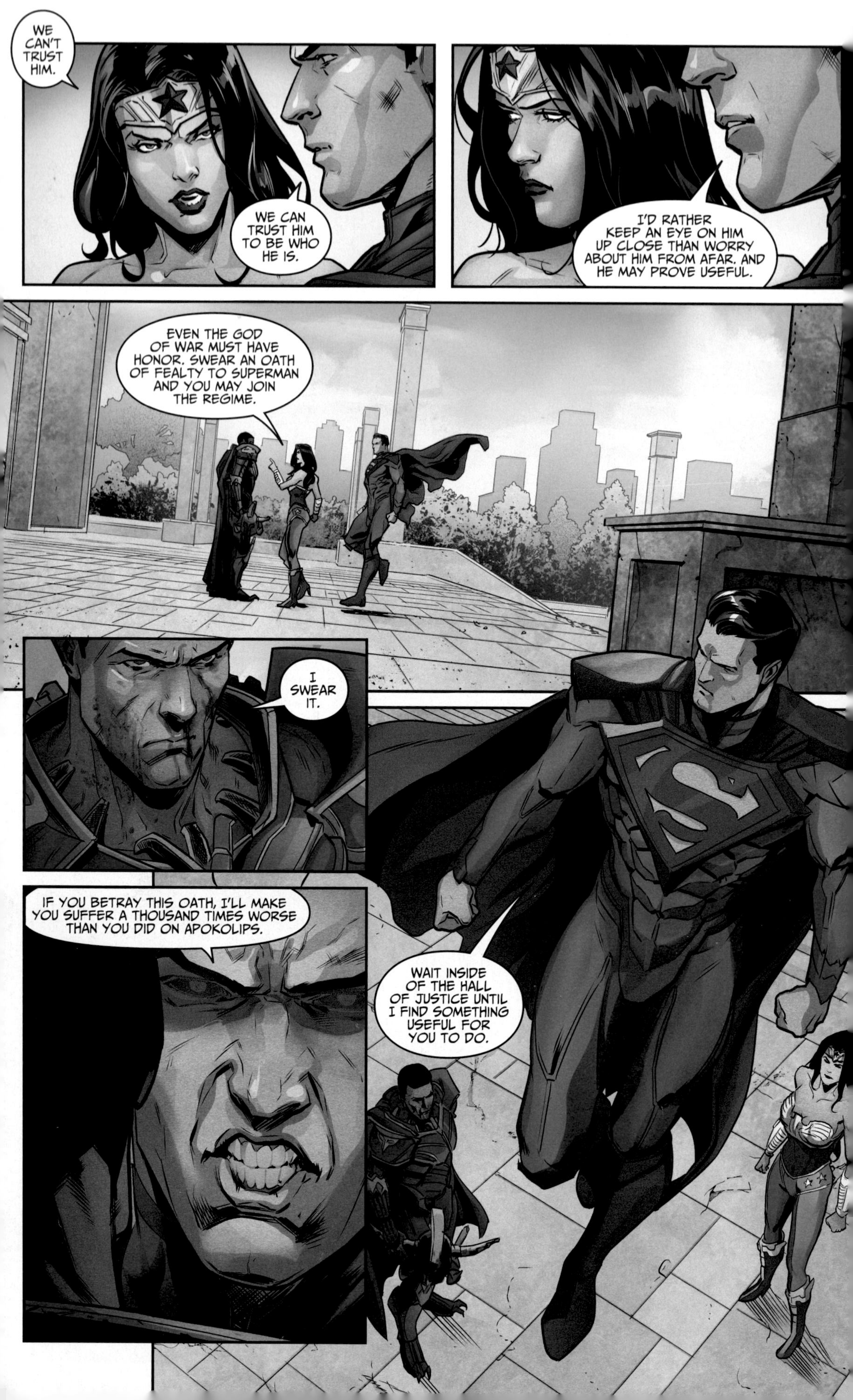
WE CAN'T TRUST HIM.
WE CAN TRUST HIM TO BE WHO HE IS.
I'D RATHER KEEP AN EYE ON HIM UP CLOSE THAN WORRY ABOUT HIM FROM AFAR. AND HE MAY PROVE USEFUL.
EVEN THE GOD OF WAR MUST HAVE HONOR. SWEAR AN OATH OF FEALTY TO SUPERMAN AND YOU MAY JOIN THE REGIME.
I SWEAR IT.
IF YOU BETRAY THIS OATH, I'LL MAKE YOU SUFFER A THOUSAND TIMES WORSE THAN YOU DID ON APOKOLIPS.
WAIT INSIDE OF THE HALL OF JUSTICE UNTIL I FIND SOMETHING USEFUL FOR YOU TO DO.

THE END

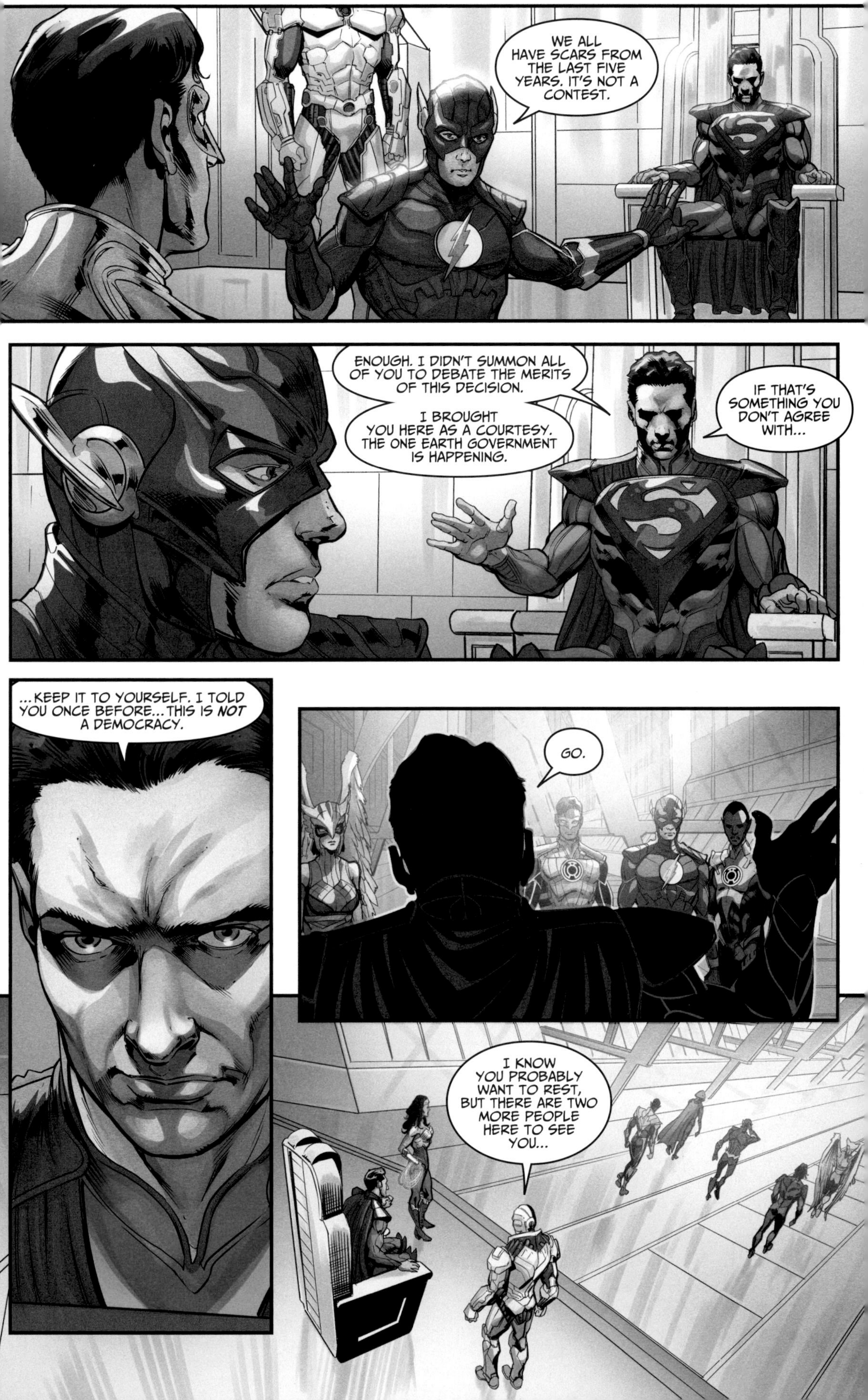
WE ALL HAVE SCARS FROM THE LAST FIVE YEARS. IT'S NOT A CONTEST.
ENOUGH. I DIDN'T SUMMON ALL OF YOU TO DEBATE THE MERITS OF THIS DECISION.
I BROUGHT YOU HERE AS A COURTESY. THE ONE EARTH GOVERNMENT IS HAPPENING.
IF THAT'S SOMETHING YOU DON'T AGREE WITH...
...KEEP IT TO YOURSELF. I TOLD YOU ONCE BEFORE... THIS IS *NOT* A DEMOCRACY.
GO.
I KNOW YOU PROBABLY WANT TO REST, BUT THERE ARE TWO MORE PEOPLE HERE TO SEE YOU...

ALL SYSTEMS CHECK. WE ARE STANDING BY FOR YOUR MARK, JEFFERSON...

IF SOMETHING GOES WRONG, HAL, WE'RE GOING TO NEED YOU TO STEP IN.

ABSOLUTELY. SO HOW DOES THIS WORK?

THERE'S A LOT OF COMPLEX SCIENCE INVOLVED... I'M NOT SURE I CAN ROBUSTLY EXPLAIN IT IN LAYMAN'S TERMS, BUT I WILL TRY...

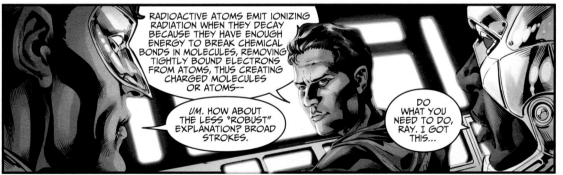

RADIOACTIVE ATOMS EMIT IONIZING RADIATION WHEN THEY DECAY BECAUSE THEY HAVE ENOUGH ENERGY TO BREAK CHEMICAL BONDS IN MOLECULES, REMOVING TIGHTLY BOUND ELECTRONS FROM ATOMS, THUS CREATING CHARGED MOLECULES OR ATOMS--

UM. HOW ABOUT THE LESS "ROBUST" EXPLANATION? BROAD STROKES.

DO WHAT YOU NEED TO DO, RAY. I GOT THIS...

JEFFERSON, IT'S SHOWTIME.

I'M READY. LET'S FIRE IT UP.

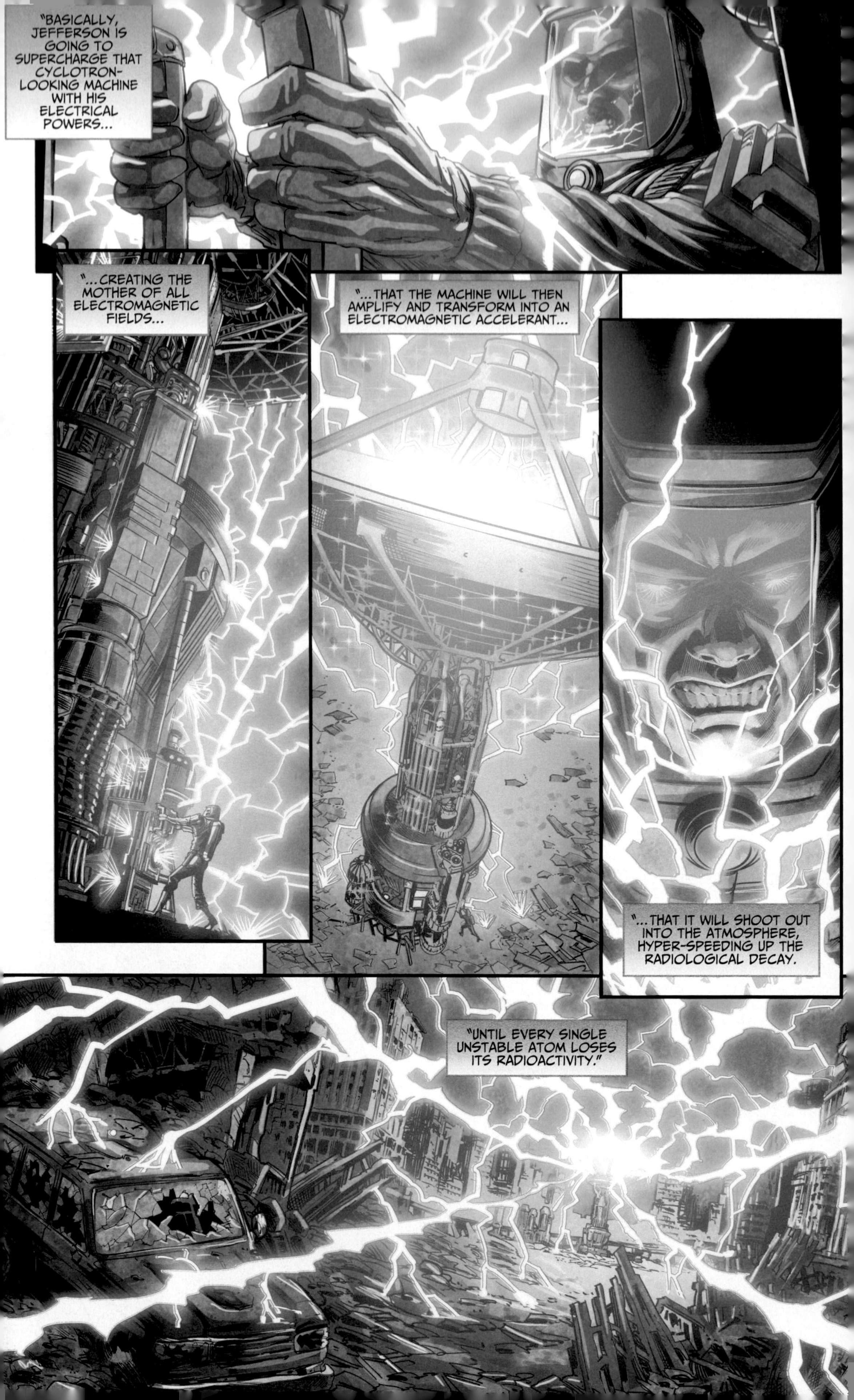
"BASICALLY, JEFFERSON IS GOING TO SUPERCHARGE THAT CYCLOTRON-LOOKING MACHINE WITH HIS ELECTRICAL POWERS...
"...CREATING THE MOTHER OF ALL ELECTROMAGNETIC FIELDS...
"...THAT THE MACHINE WILL THEN AMPLIFY AND TRANSFORM INTO AN ELECTROMAGNETIC ACCELERANT...
"...THAT IT WILL SHOOT OUT INTO THE ATMOSPHERE, HYPER-SPEEDING UP THE RADIOLOGICAL DECAY.
"UNTIL EVERY SINGLE UNSTABLE ATOM LOSES ITS RADIOACTIVITY."

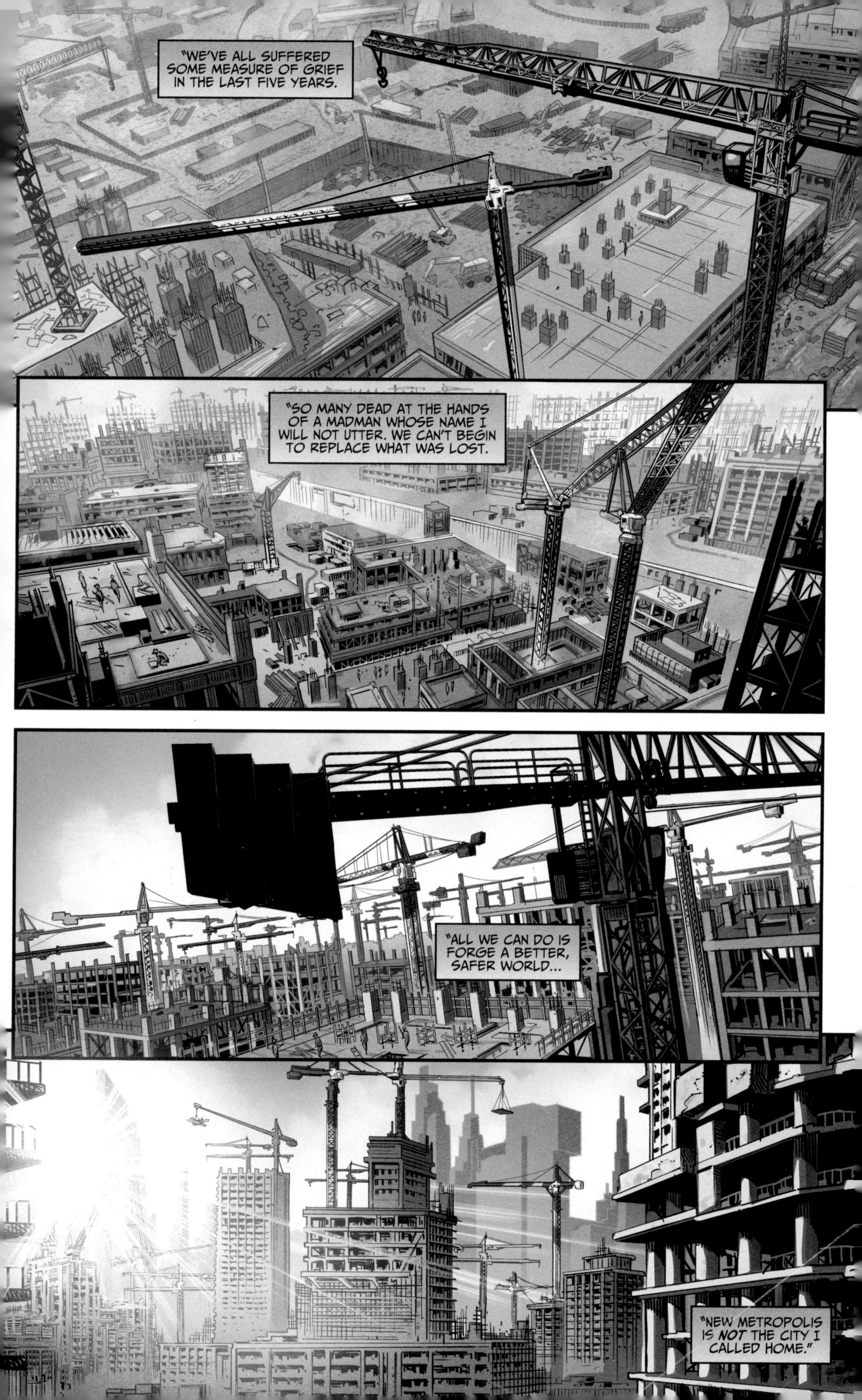
"WE'VE ALL SUFFERED SOME MEASURE OF GRIEF IN THE LAST FIVE YEARS.
"SO MANY DEAD AT THE HANDS OF A MADMAN WHOSE NAME I WILL NOT UTTER. WE CAN'T BEGIN TO REPLACE WHAT WAS LOST.
"ALL WE CAN DO IS FORGE A BETTER, SAFER WORLD...
"NEW METROPOLIS IS *NOT* THE CITY I CALLED HOME."

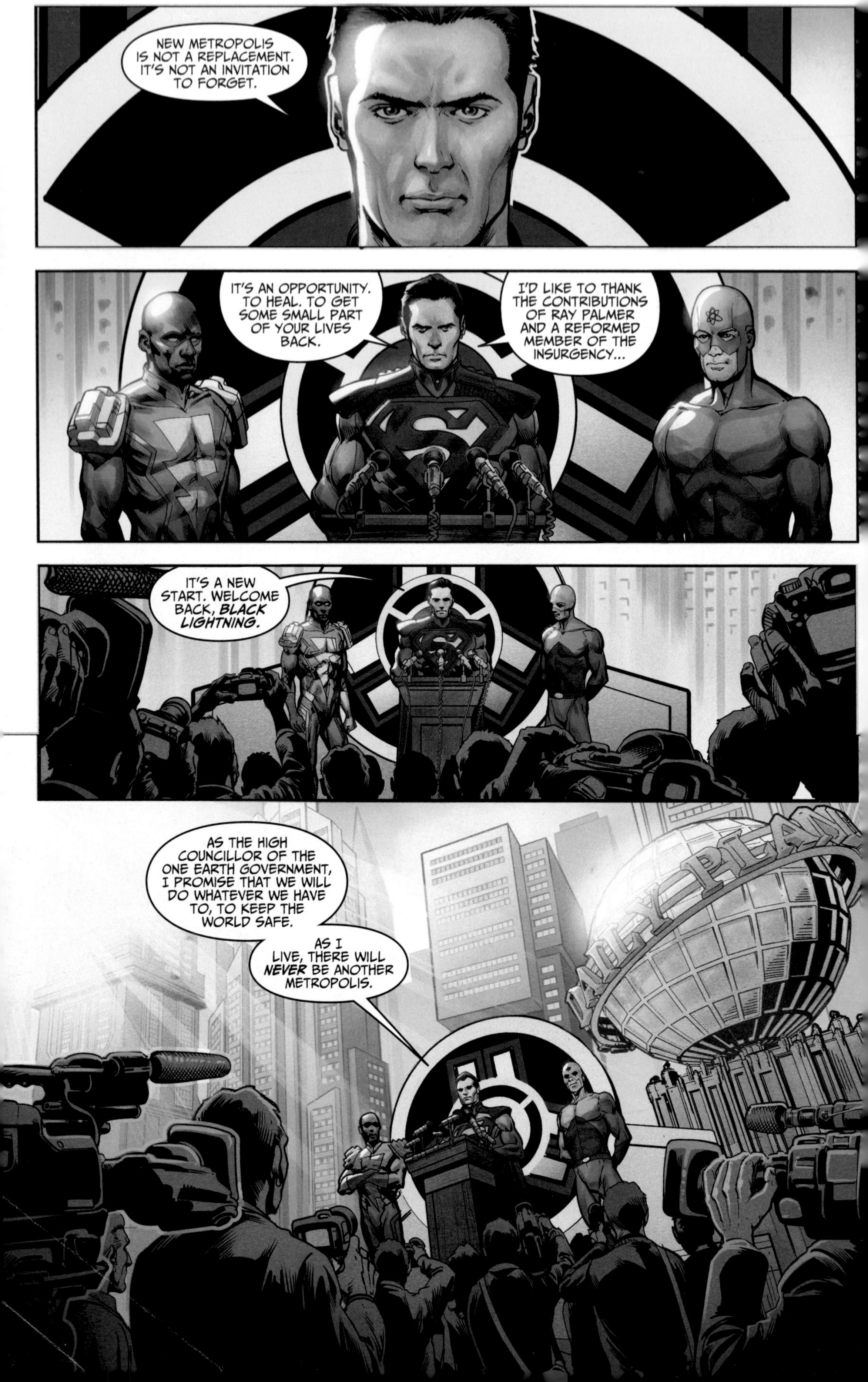
NEW METROPOLIS IS NOT A REPLACEMENT. IT'S NOT AN INVITATION TO FORGET.
IT'S AN OPPORTUNITY. TO HEAL. TO GET SOME SMALL PART OF YOUR LIVES BACK.
I'D LIKE TO THANK THE CONTRIBUTIONS OF RAY PALMER AND A REFORMED MEMBER OF THE INSURGENCY...
IT'S A NEW START. WELCOME BACK, *BLACK LIGHTNING.*
AS THE HIGH COUNCILLOR OF THE ONE EARTH GOVERNMENT, I PROMISE THAT WE WILL DO WHATEVER WE HAVE TO, TO KEEP THE WORLD SAFE.
AS I LIVE, THERE WILL *NEVER* BE ANOTHER METROPOLIS.

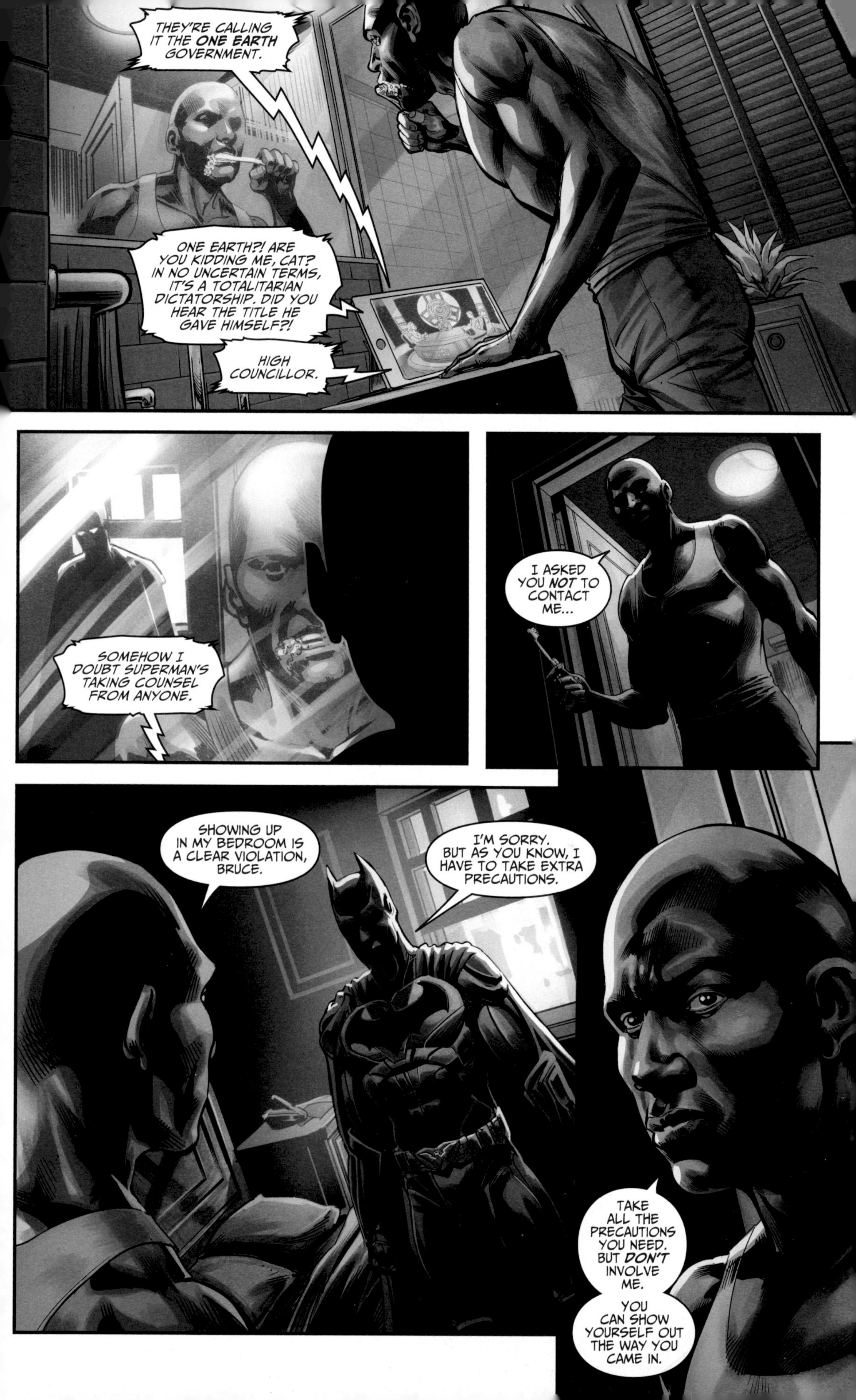
THEY'RE CALLING IT THE ONE EARTH GOVERNMENT.
ONE EARTH?! ARE YOU KIDDING ME, CAT? IN NO UNCERTAIN TERMS, IT'S A TOTALITARIAN DICTATORSHIP. DID YOU HEAR THE TITLE HE GAVE HIMSELF?!
HIGH COUNCILLOR.
SOMEHOW I DOUBT SUPERMAN'S TAKING COUNSEL FROM ANYONE.
I ASKED YOU NOT TO CONTACT ME...
SHOWING UP IN MY BEDROOM IS A CLEAR VIOLATION, BRUCE.
I'M SORRY. BUT AS YOU KNOW, I HAVE TO TAKE EXTRA PRECAUTIONS.
TAKE ALL THE PRECAUTIONS YOU NEED. BUT DON'T INVOLVE ME.
YOU CAN SHOW YOURSELF OUT THE WAY YOU CAME IN.

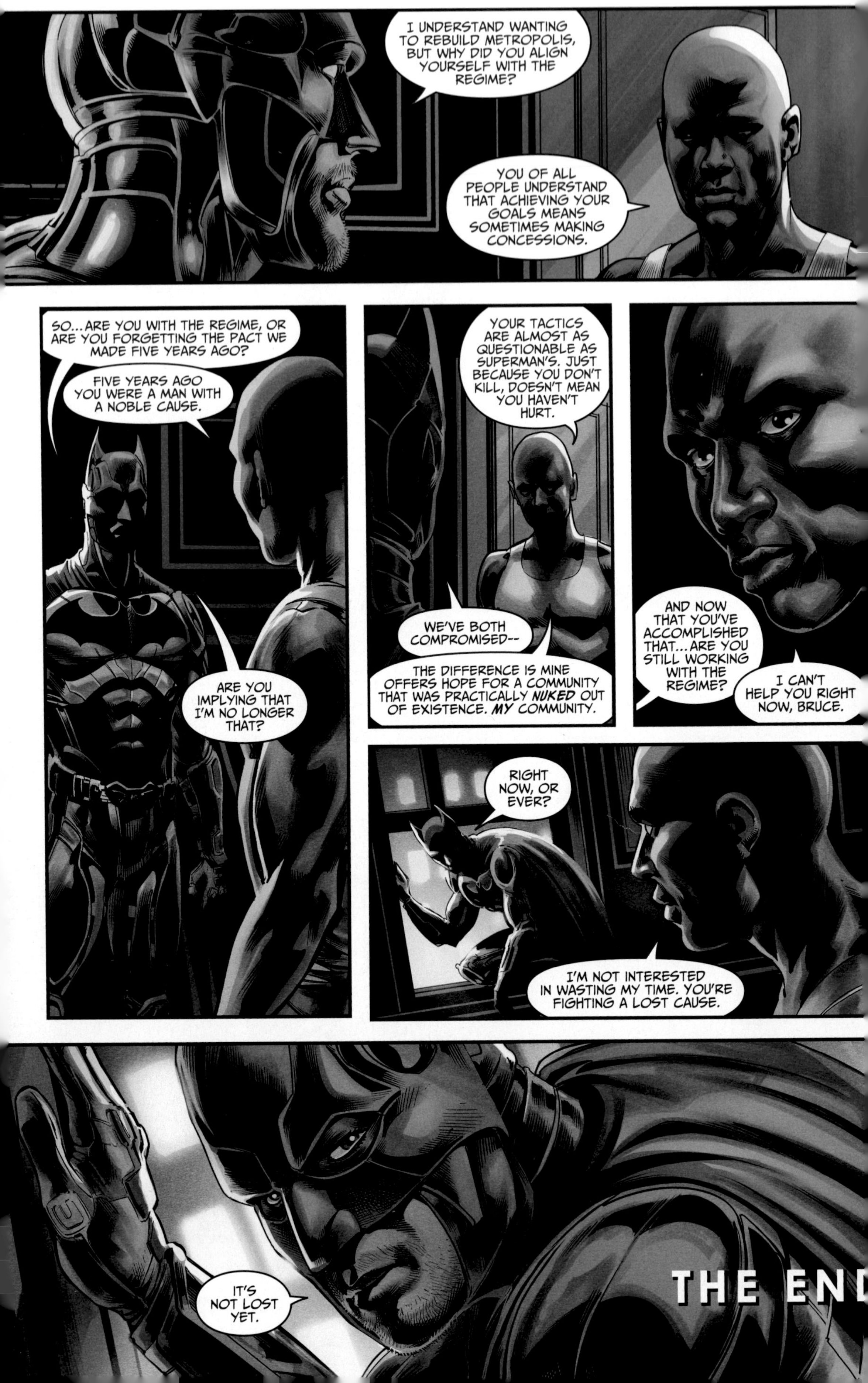
I UNDERSTAND WANTING TO REBUILD METROPOLIS, BUT WHY DID YOU ALIGN YOURSELF WITH THE REGIME?
YOU OF ALL PEOPLE UNDERSTAND THAT ACHIEVING YOUR GOALS MEANS SOMETIMES MAKING CONCESSIONS.
SO...ARE YOU WITH THE REGIME, OR ARE YOU FORGETTING THE PACT WE MADE FIVE YEARS AGO?
FIVE YEARS AGO YOU WERE A MAN WITH A NOBLE CAUSE.
ARE YOU IMPLYING THAT I'M NO LONGER THAT?
YOUR TACTICS ARE ALMOST AS QUESTIONABLE AS SUPERMAN'S. JUST BECAUSE YOU DON'T KILL, DOESN'T MEAN YOU HAVEN'T HURT.
WE'VE BOTH COMPROMISED--
THE DIFFERENCE IS MINE OFFERS HOPE FOR A COMMUNITY THAT WAS PRACTICALLY *NUKED* OUT OF EXISTENCE. *MY* COMMUNITY.
AND NOW THAT YOU'VE ACCOMPLISHED THAT...ARE YOU STILL WORKING WITH THE REGIME?
I CAN'T HELP YOU RIGHT NOW, BRUCE.
RIGHT NOW, OR EVER?
I'M NOT INTERESTED IN WASTING MY TIME. YOU'RE FIGHTING A LOST CAUSE.
IT'S NOT LOST YET.
THE END

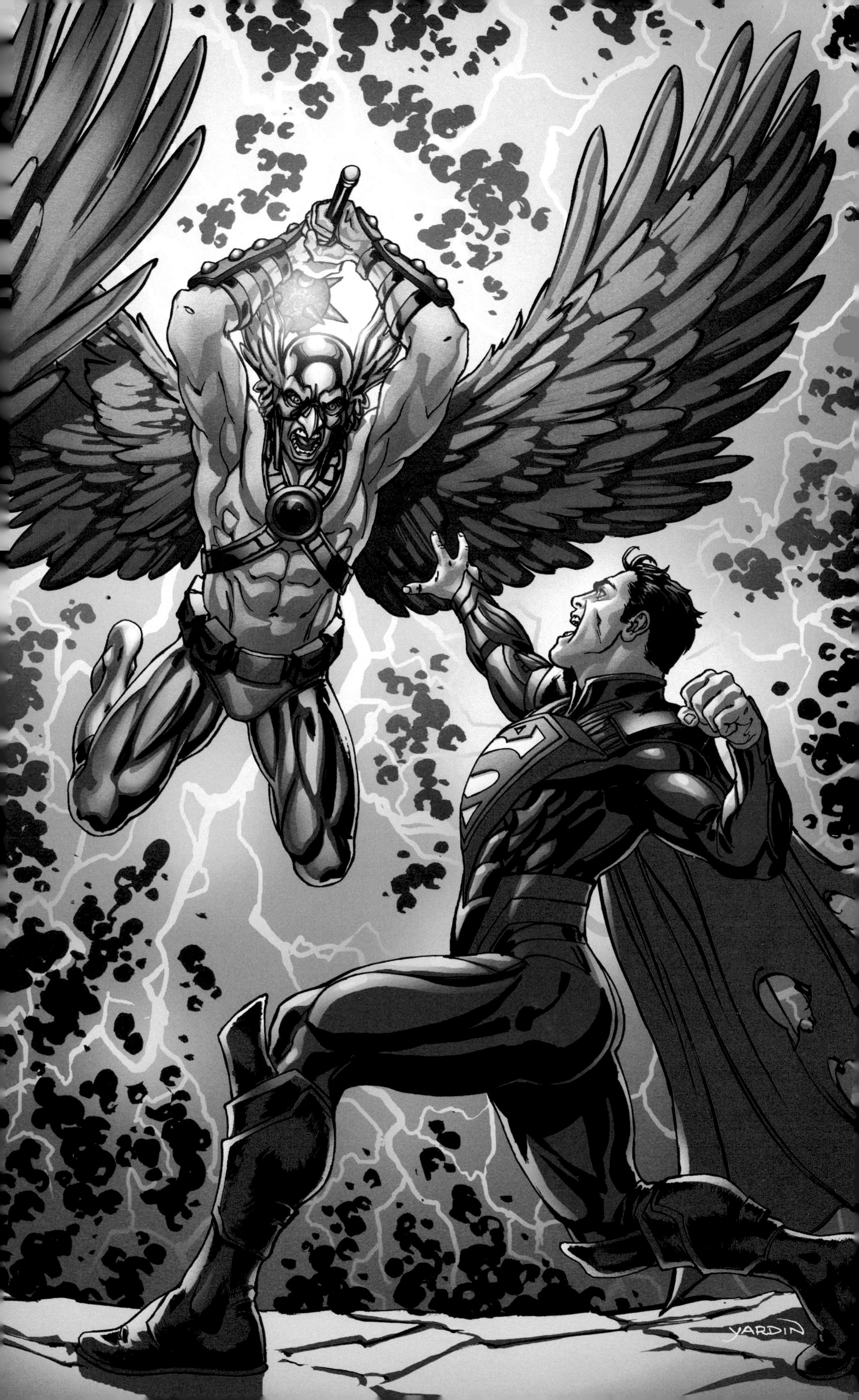
YARDIN

"Thrones" **Xermanico** Artist **Rex Lokus** Colorist

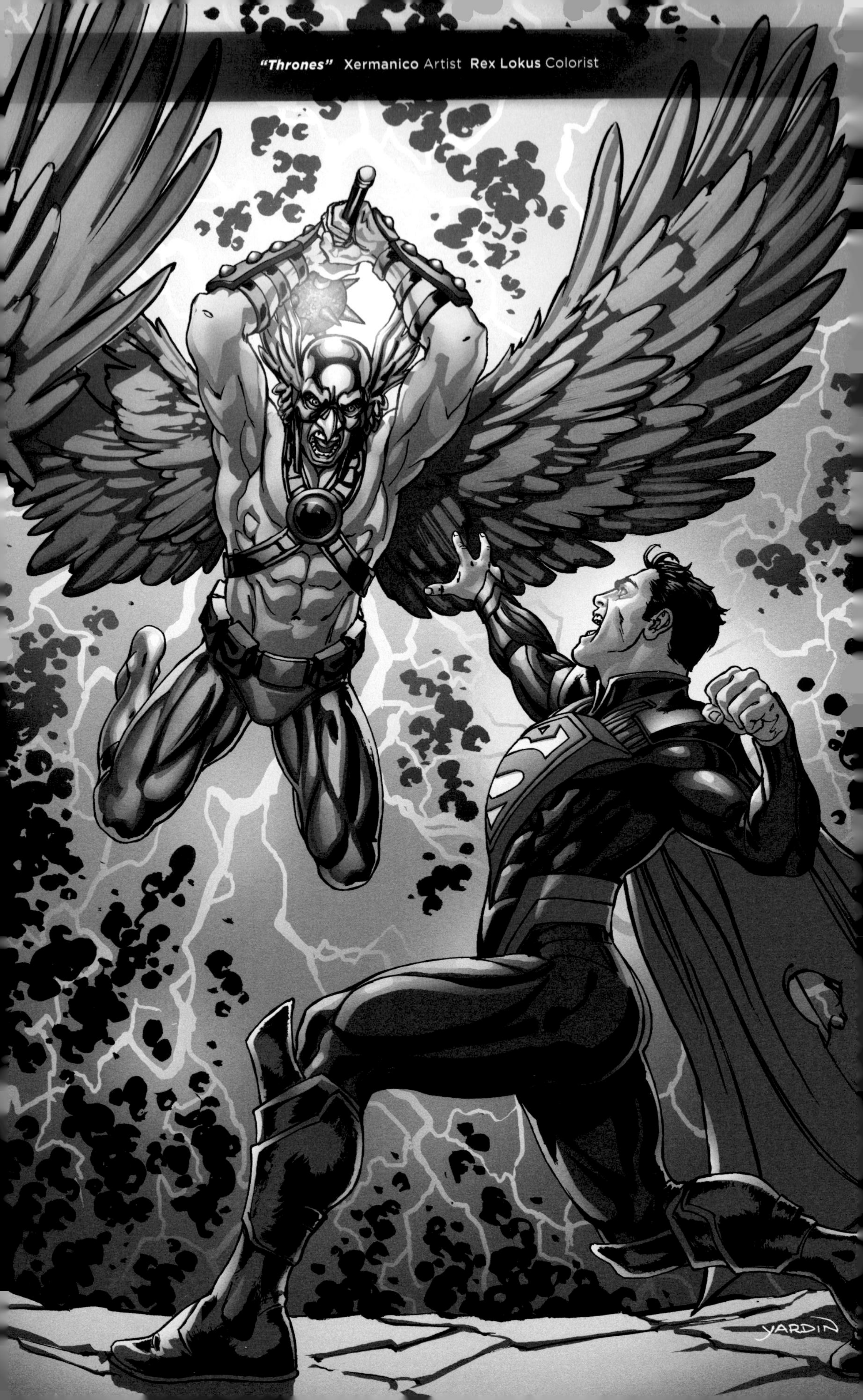
YARDIN

THRONES

THE PACIFIC LEAD MINES, NORTHWEST ALASKA.

BRUCE...

YES, BARBARA?

WE ARE WELL PAST PEP TALKS AND RALLYING THE TROOPS. IT'S TIME FOR REAL TALK...

REAL TALK?

JUST BETWEEN US. NO JUDGMENTS. NO BLAME. ARE THERE ANY MORE PLANS? SOME DARING GAMBIT TO SNATCH VICTORY FROM THE JAWS OF DEFEAT? BE HONEST...

IS IT OVER?

BARBARA...

IT'S NOT OVER.

GOOD.

BATMAN...

I NEED TO SEND A SECURE TRANSMISSION.

WHERE?

BEYOND SECTOR 2814.

THAT'S GOING TO BE HARD TO DO WITH CYBORG MONITORING EVERY TRANSMISSION, BROADCAST AND SATELLITE ON THE PLANET.

HARD, BUT NOT IMPOSSIBLE?

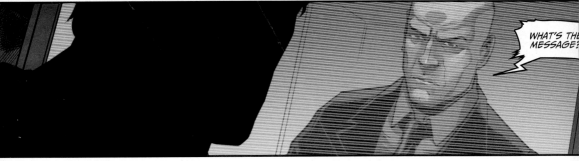

WHAT'S THE MESSAGE?

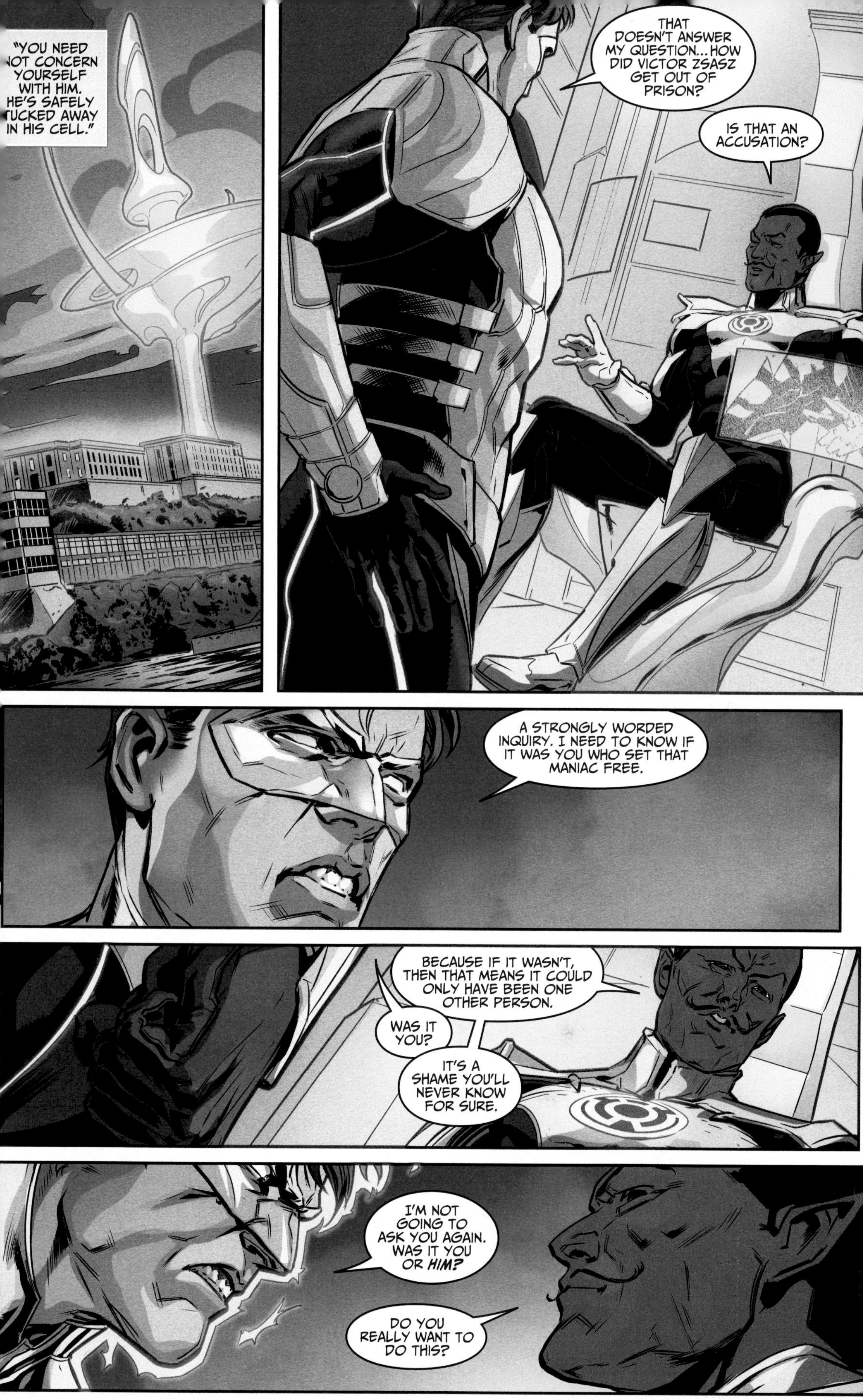
"YOU NEED NOT CONCERN YOURSELF WITH HIM. HE'S SAFELY TUCKED AWAY IN HIS CELL."
THAT DOESN'T ANSWER MY QUESTION... HOW DID VICTOR ZSASZ GET OUT OF PRISON?
IS THAT AN ACCUSATION?
A STRONGLY WORDED INQUIRY. I NEED TO KNOW IF IT WAS YOU WHO SET THAT MANIAC FREE.
BECAUSE IF IT WASN'T, THEN THAT MEANS IT COULD ONLY HAVE BEEN ONE OTHER PERSON.
WAS IT YOU?
IT'S A SHAME YOU'LL NEVER KNOW FOR SURE.
I'M NOT GOING TO ASK YOU AGAIN. WAS IT YOU OR *HIM?*
DO YOU REALLY WANT TO DO THIS?

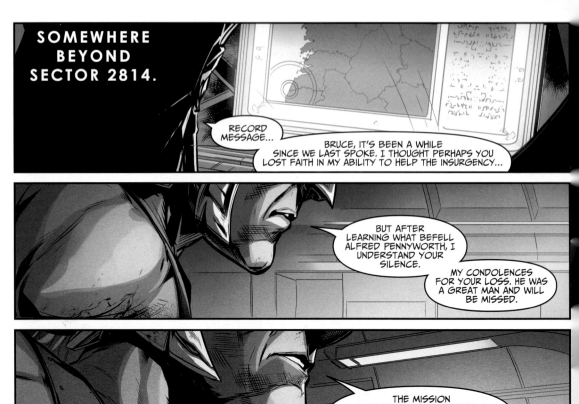

SOMEWHERE
BEYOND
SECTOR 2814.

RECORD MESSAGE...

BRUCE, IT'S BEEN A WHILE SINCE WE LAST SPOKE. I THOUGHT PERHAPS YOU LOST FAITH IN MY ABILITY TO HELP THE INSURGENCY...

BUT AFTER LEARNING WHAT BEFELL ALFRED PENNYWORTH, I UNDERSTAND YOUR SILENCE.

MY CONDOLENCES FOR YOUR LOSS. HE WAS A GREAT MAN AND WILL BE MISSED.

THE MISSION YOU TASKED ME IS FINALLY PROGRESSING. AFTER CONSIDERABLE EFFORT, I HAVE LOCATED THE OBJECTIVE.

I'M ON MY WAY TO RETRIEVE IT...

NOTHING WILL STOP ME FROM GETTING IT.

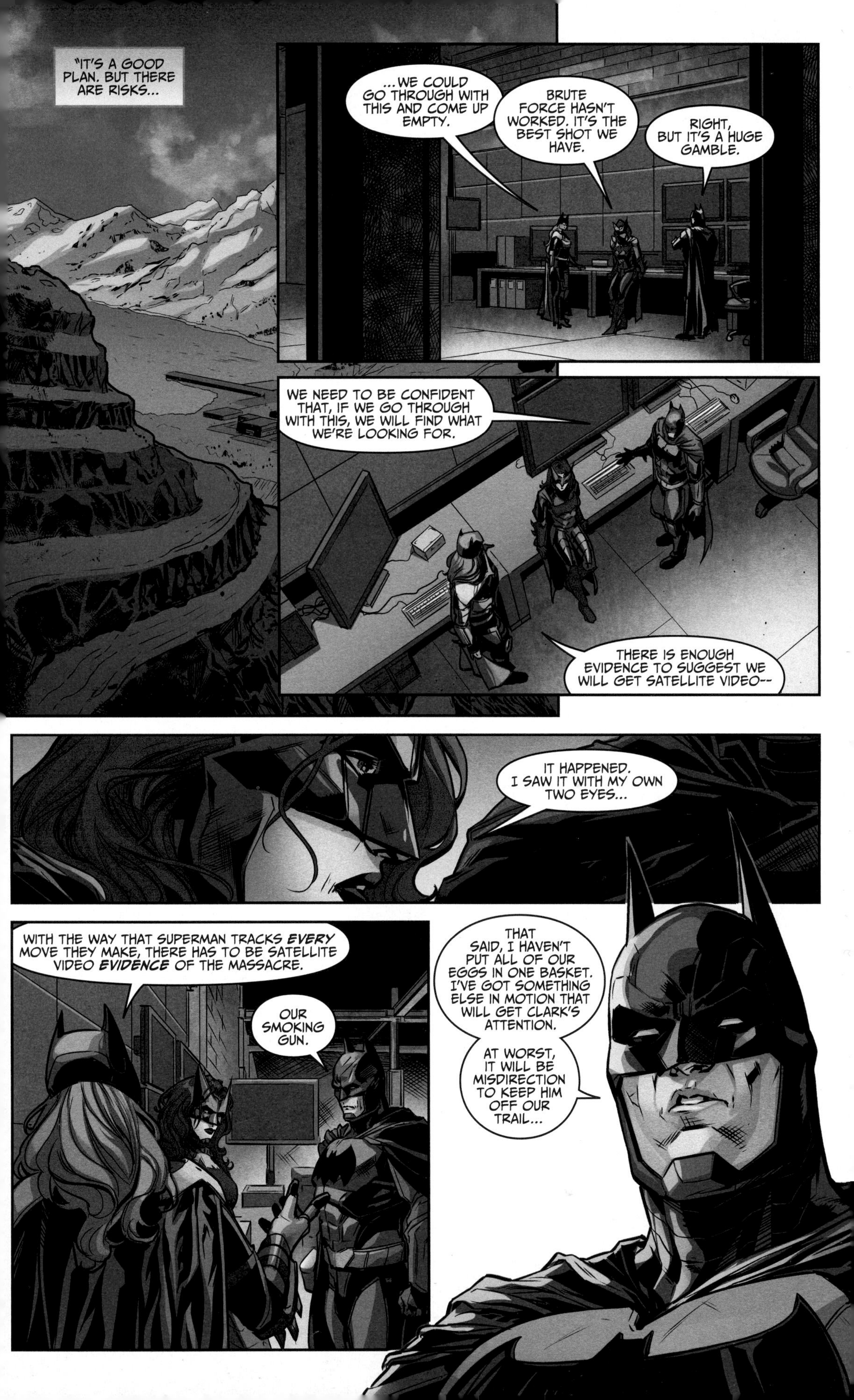
"IT'S A GOOD PLAN. BUT THERE ARE RISKS...
...WE COULD GO THROUGH WITH THIS AND COME UP EMPTY.
BRUTE FORCE HASN'T WORKED. IT'S THE BEST SHOT WE HAVE.
RIGHT, BUT IT'S A HUGE GAMBLE.
WE NEED TO BE CONFIDENT THAT, IF WE GO THROUGH WITH THIS, WE WILL FIND WHAT WE'RE LOOKING FOR.
THERE IS ENOUGH EVIDENCE TO SUGGEST WE WILL GET SATELLITE VIDEO--
IT HAPPENED. I SAW IT WITH MY OWN TWO EYES...
WITH THE WAY THAT SUPERMAN TRACKS *EVERY* MOVE THEY MAKE, THERE HAS TO BE SATELLITE VIDEO *EVIDENCE* OF THE MASSACRE.
OUR SMOKING GUN.
THAT SAID, I HAVEN'T PUT ALL OF OUR EGGS IN ONE BASKET. I'VE GOT SOMETHING ELSE IN MOTION THAT WILL GET CLARK'S ATTENTION.
AT WORST, IT WILL BE MISDIRECTION TO KEEP HIM OFF OUR TRAIL...

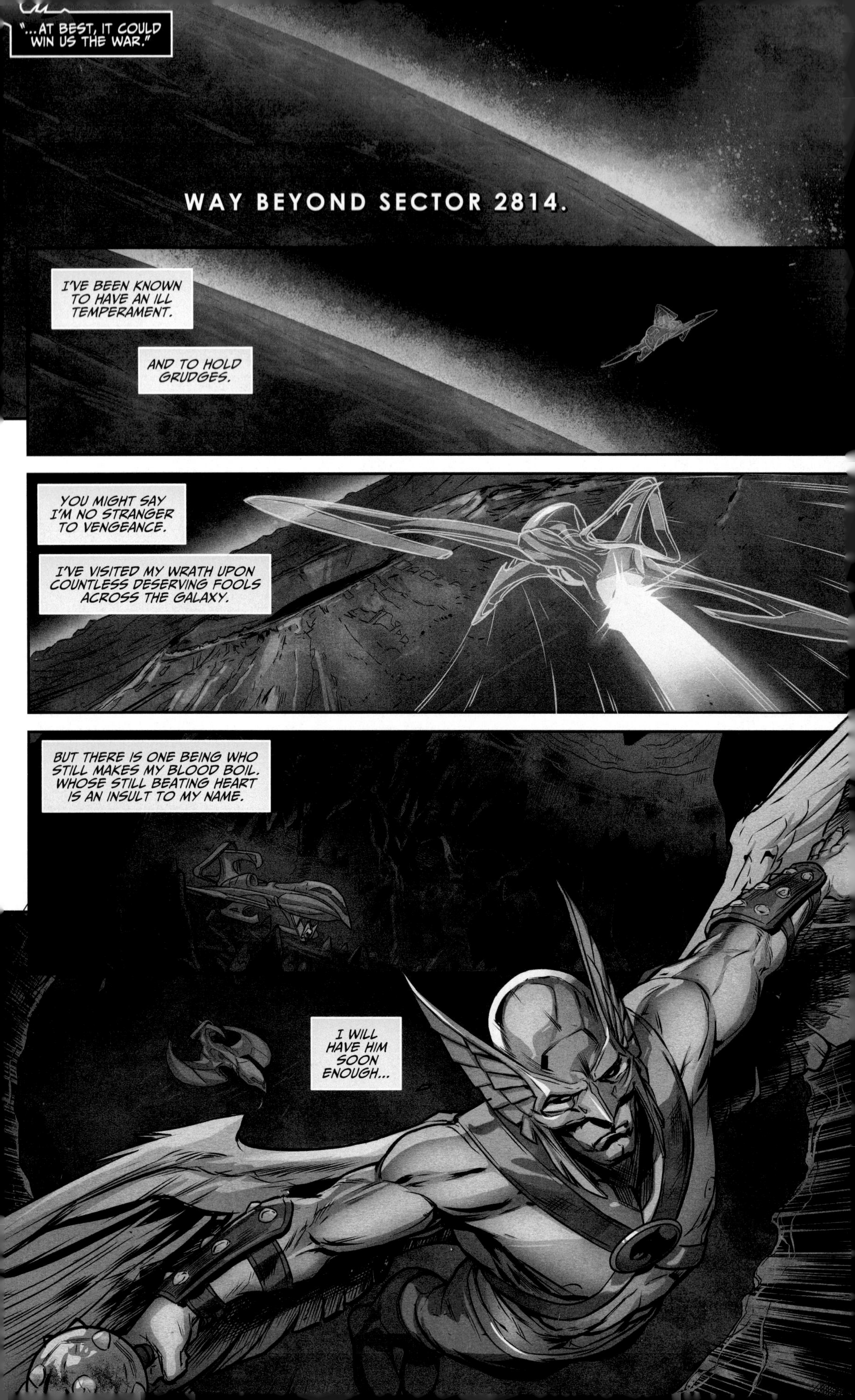
"...AT BEST, IT COULD WIN US THE WAR."
WAY BEYOND SECTOR 2814.
I'VE BEEN KNOWN TO HAVE AN ILL TEMPERAMENT.
AND TO HOLD GRUDGES.
YOU MIGHT SAY I'M NO STRANGER TO VENGEANCE.
I'VE VISITED MY WRATH UPON COUNTLESS DESERVING FOOLS ACROSS THE GALAXY.
BUT THERE IS ONE BEING WHO STILL MAKES MY BLOOD BOIL. WHOSE STILL BEATING HEART IS AN INSULT TO MY NAME.
I WILL HAVE HIM SOON ENOUGH...

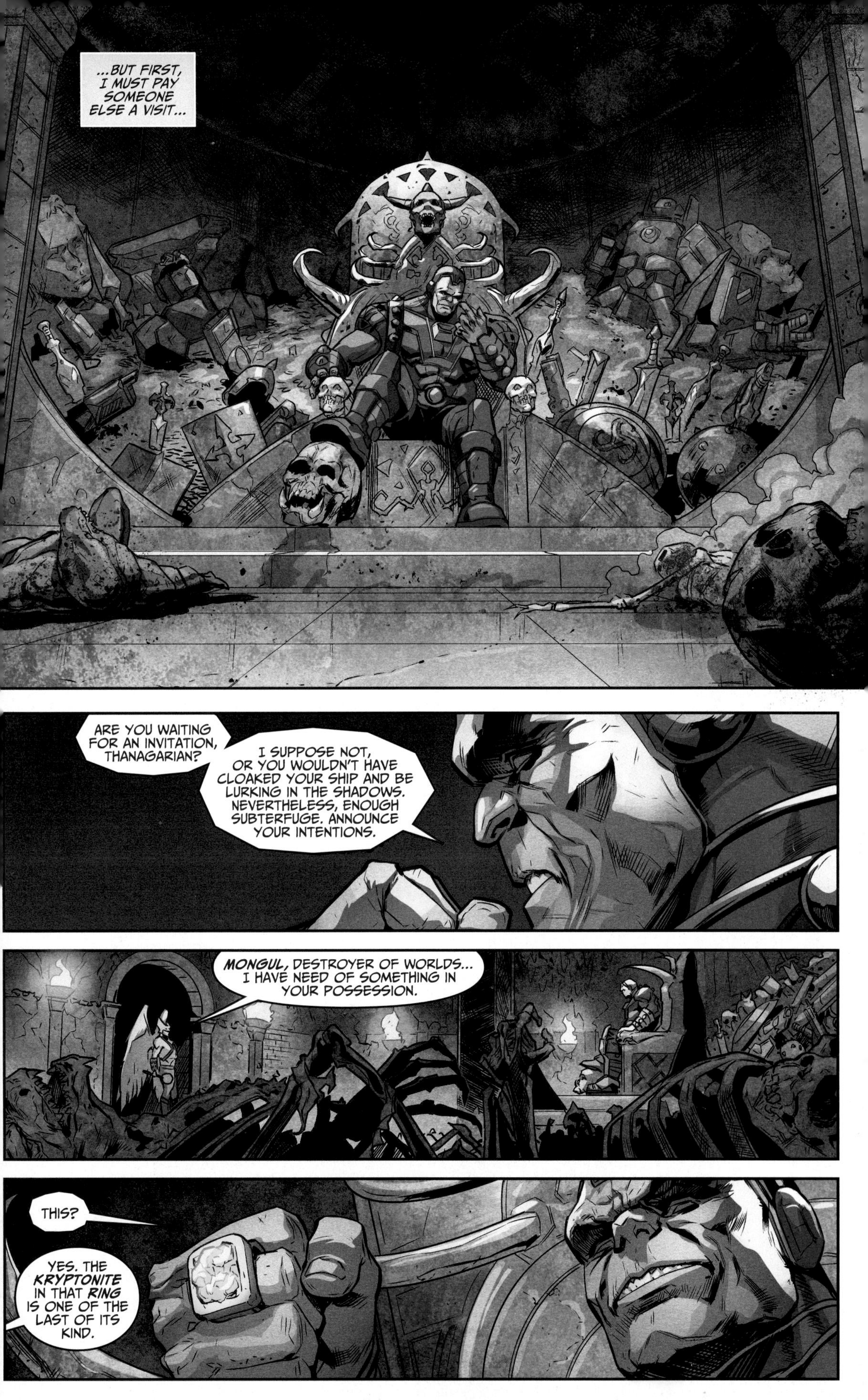
...BUT FIRST, I MUST PAY SOMEONE ELSE A VISIT...
ARE YOU WAITING FOR AN INVITATION, THANAGARIAN?
I SUPPOSE NOT, OR YOU WOULDN'T HAVE CLOAKED YOUR SHIP AND BE LURKING IN THE SHADOWS. NEVERTHELESS, ENOUGH SUBTERFUGE. ANNOUNCE YOUR INTENTIONS.
MONGUL, DESTROYER OF WORLDS... I HAVE NEED OF SOMETHING IN YOUR POSSESSION.
THIS?
YES. THE KRYPTONITE IN THAT RING IS ONE OF THE LAST OF ITS KIND.

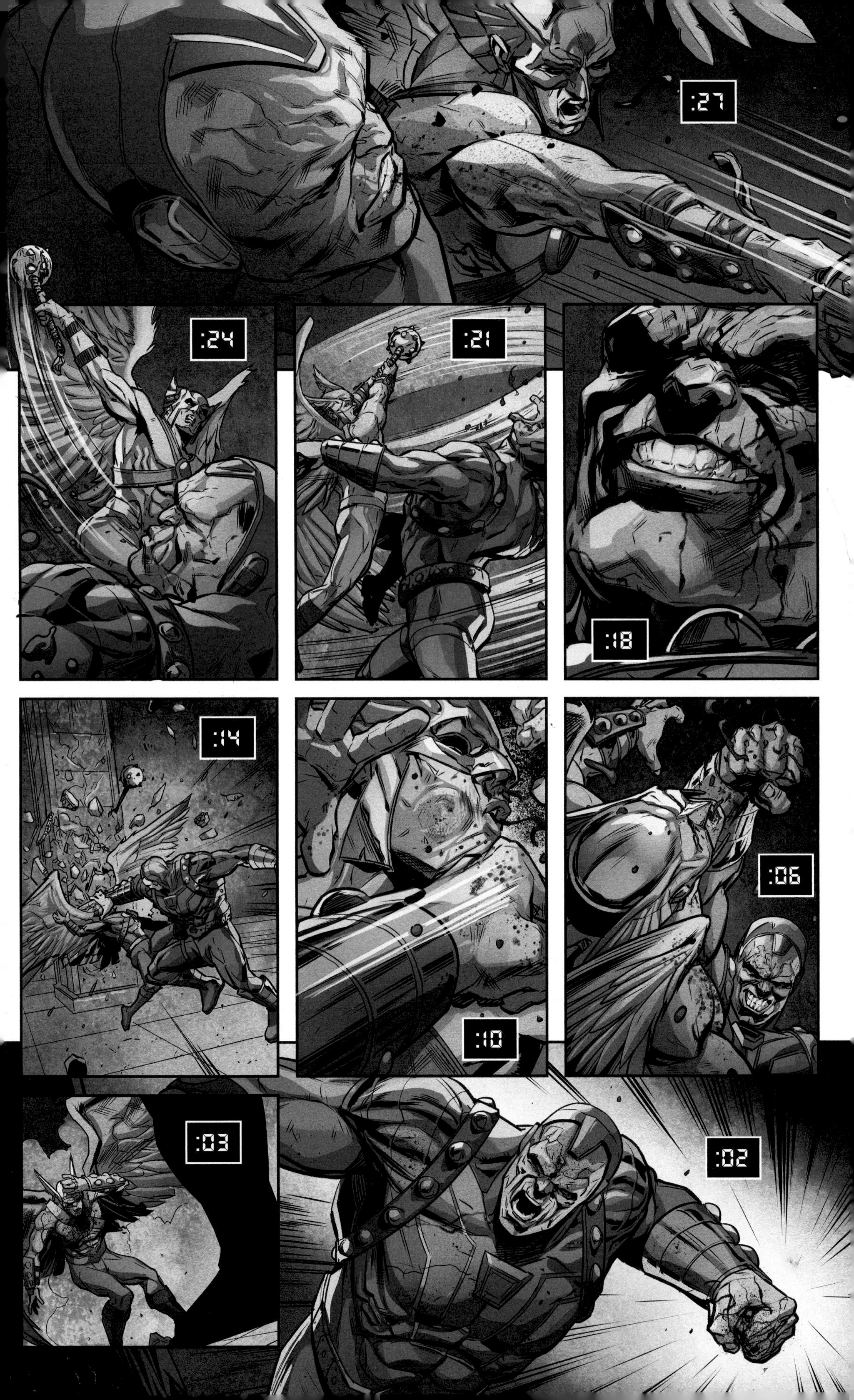
:27
:24
:21
:18
:14
:10
:06
:03
:02

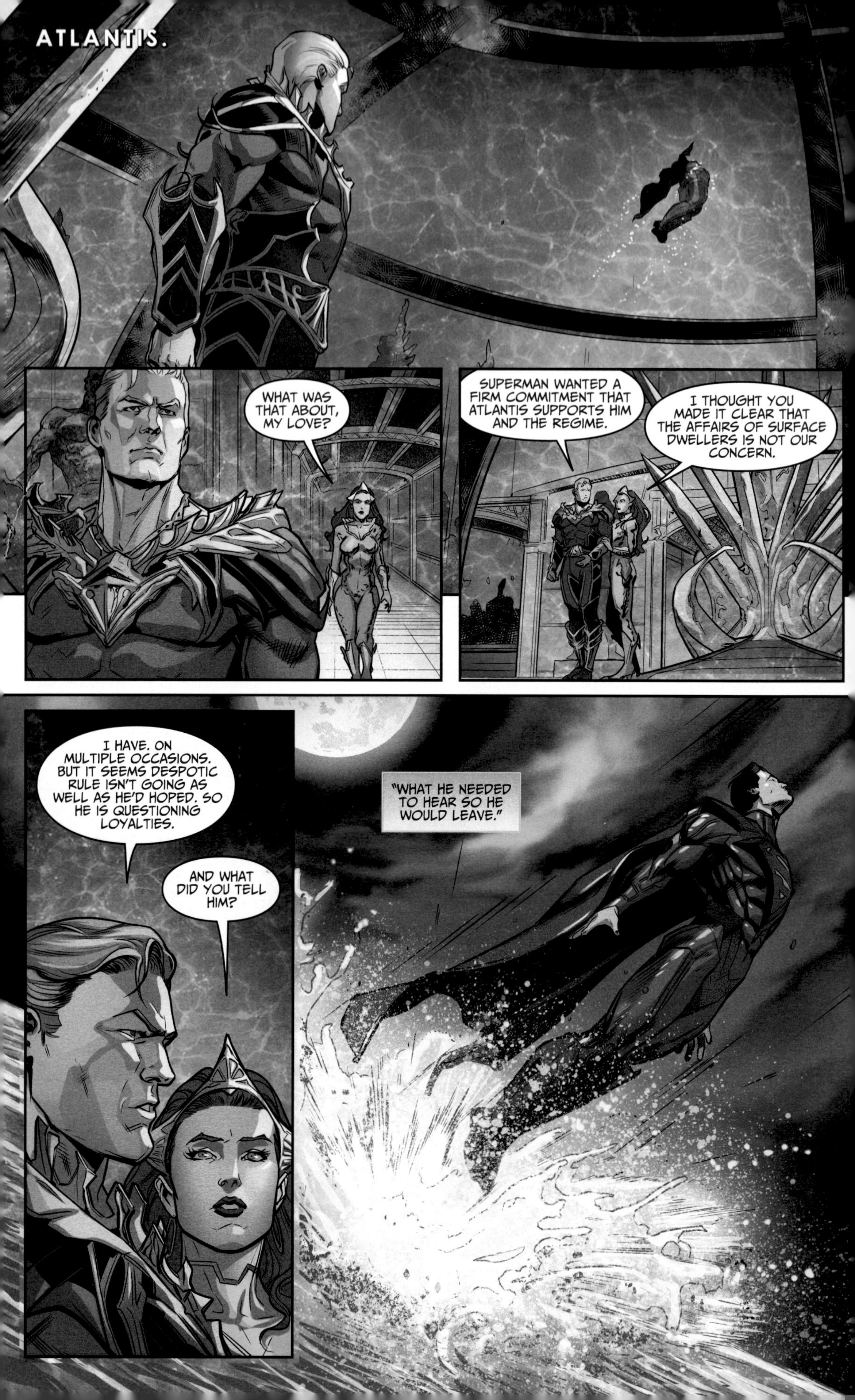
ATLANTIS.
WHAT WAS THAT ABOUT, MY LOVE?
SUPERMAN WANTED A FIRM COMMITMENT THAT ATLANTIS SUPPORTS HIM AND THE REGIME.
I THOUGHT YOU MADE IT CLEAR THAT THE AFFAIRS OF SURFACE DWELLERS IS NOT OUR CONCERN.
I HAVE. ON MULTIPLE OCCASIONS. BUT IT SEEMS DESPOTIC RULE ISN'T GOING AS WELL AS HE'D HOPED. SO HE IS QUESTIONING LOYALTIES.
AND WHAT DID YOU TELL HIM?
"WHAT HE NEEDED TO HEAR SO HE WOULD LEAVE."

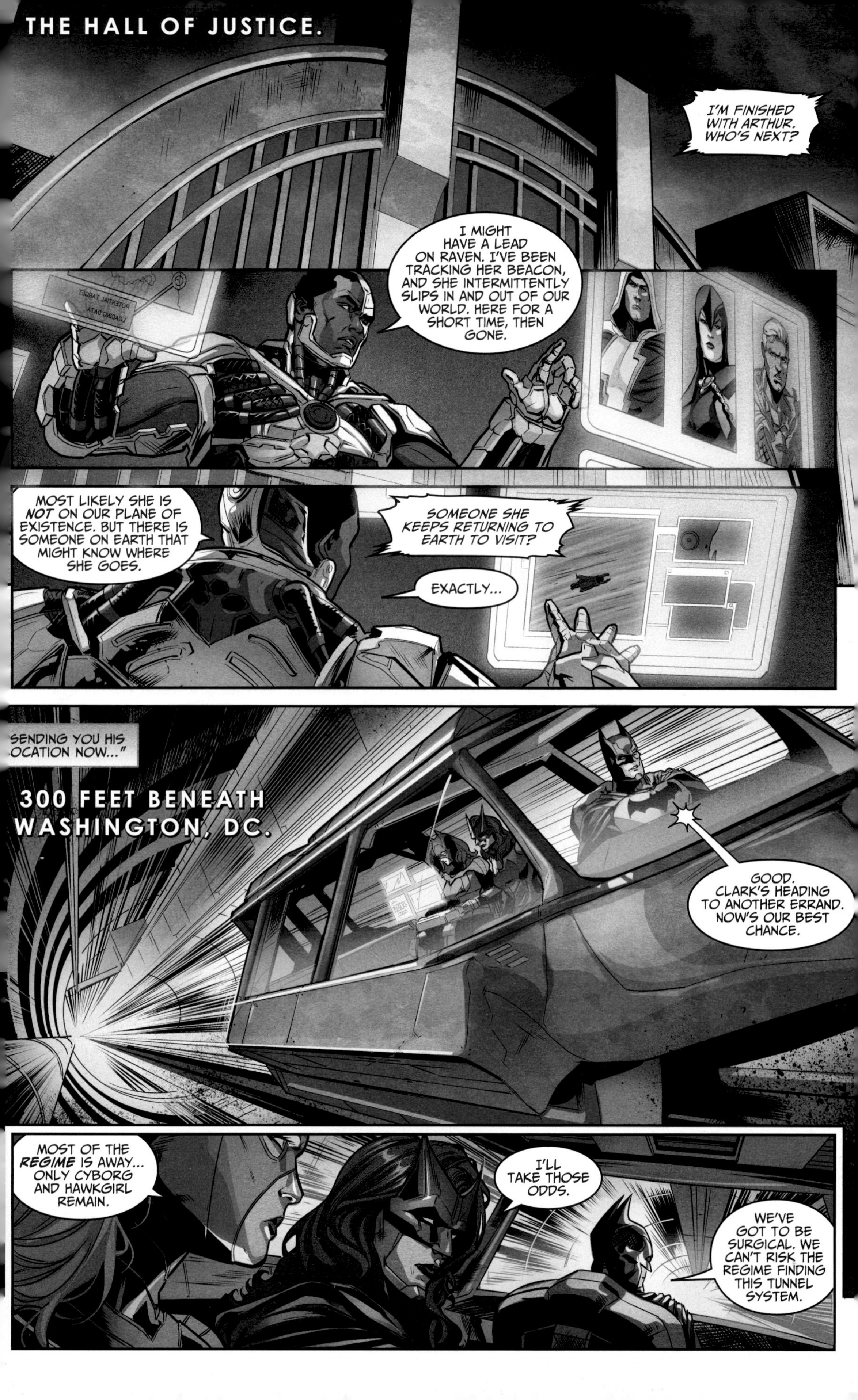
THE HALL OF JUSTICE.
I'M FINISHED WITH ARTHUR. WHO'S NEXT?
I MIGHT HAVE A LEAD ON RAVEN. I'VE BEEN TRACKING HER BEACON, AND SHE INTERMITTENTLY SLIPS IN AND OUT OF OUR WORLD. HERE FOR A SHORT TIME, THEN GONE.
MOST LIKELY SHE IS NOT ON OUR PLANE OF EXISTENCE. BUT THERE IS SOMEONE ON EARTH THAT MIGHT KNOW WHERE SHE GOES.
SOMEONE SHE KEEPS RETURNING TO EARTH TO VISIT?
EXACTLY...
SENDING YOU HIS OCATION NOW..."
300 FEET BENEATH WASHINGTON, DC.
GOOD. CLARK'S HEADING TO ANOTHER ERRAND. NOW'S OUR BEST CHANCE.
MOST OF THE REGIME IS AWAY... ONLY CYBORG AND HAWKGIRL REMAIN.
I'LL TAKE THOSE ODDS.
WE'VE GOT TO BE SURGICAL. WE CAN'T RISK THE REGIME FINDING THIS TUNNEL SYSTEM.

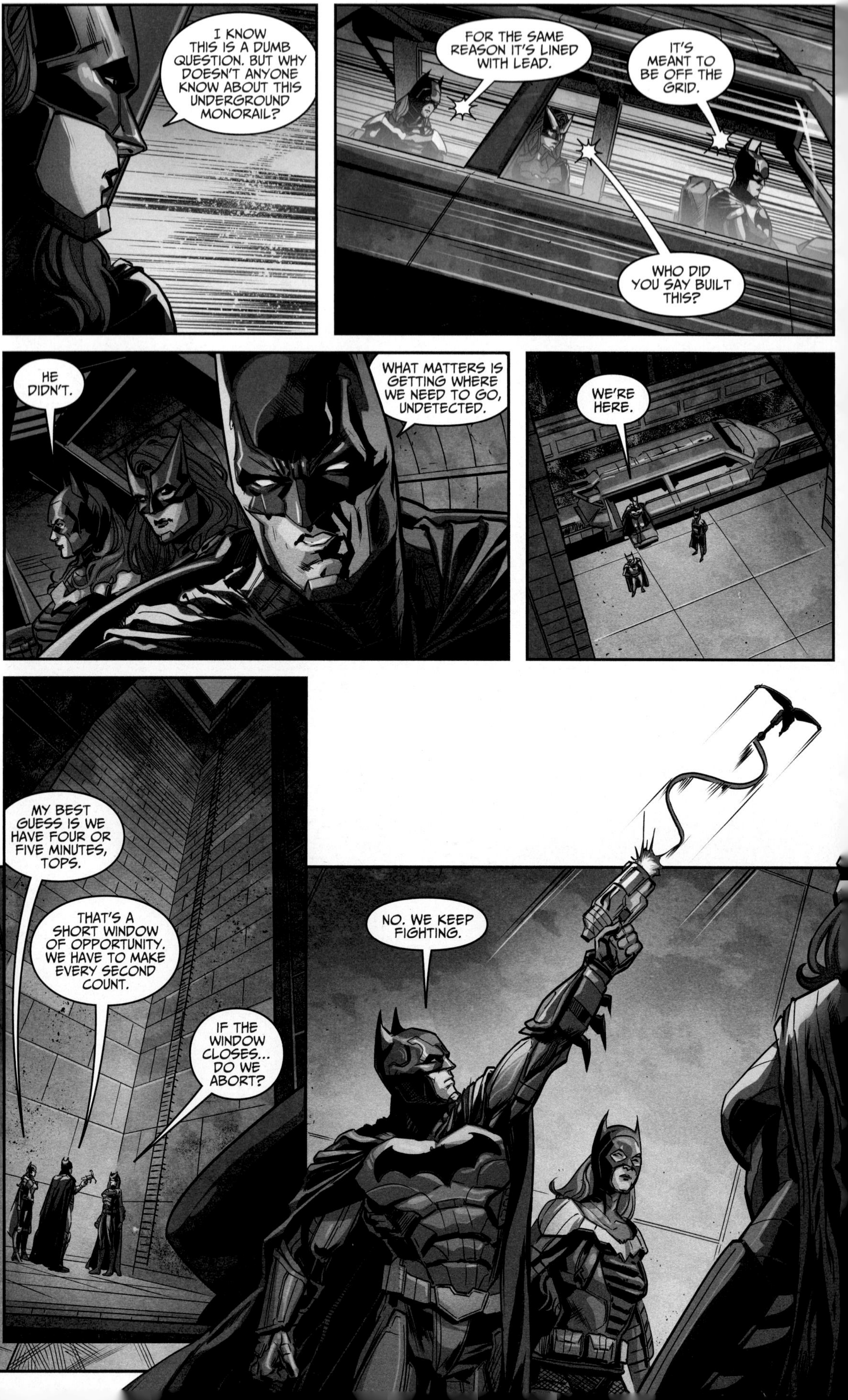

I KNOW THIS IS A DUMB QUESTION. BUT WHY DOESN'T ANYONE KNOW ABOUT THIS UNDERGROUND MONORAIL?
FOR THE SAME REASON IT'S LINED WITH LEAD.
IT'S MEANT TO BE OFF THE GRID.
WHO DID YOU SAY BUILT THIS?
HE DIDN'T.
WHAT MATTERS IS GETTING WHERE WE NEED TO GO, UNDETECTED.
WE'RE HERE.
MY BEST GUESS IS WE HAVE FOUR OR FIVE MINUTES, TOPS.
THAT'S A SHORT WINDOW OF OPPORTUNITY. WE HAVE TO MAKE EVERY SECOND COUNT.
IF THE WINDOW CLOSES... DO WE ABORT?
NO. WE KEEP FIGHTING.

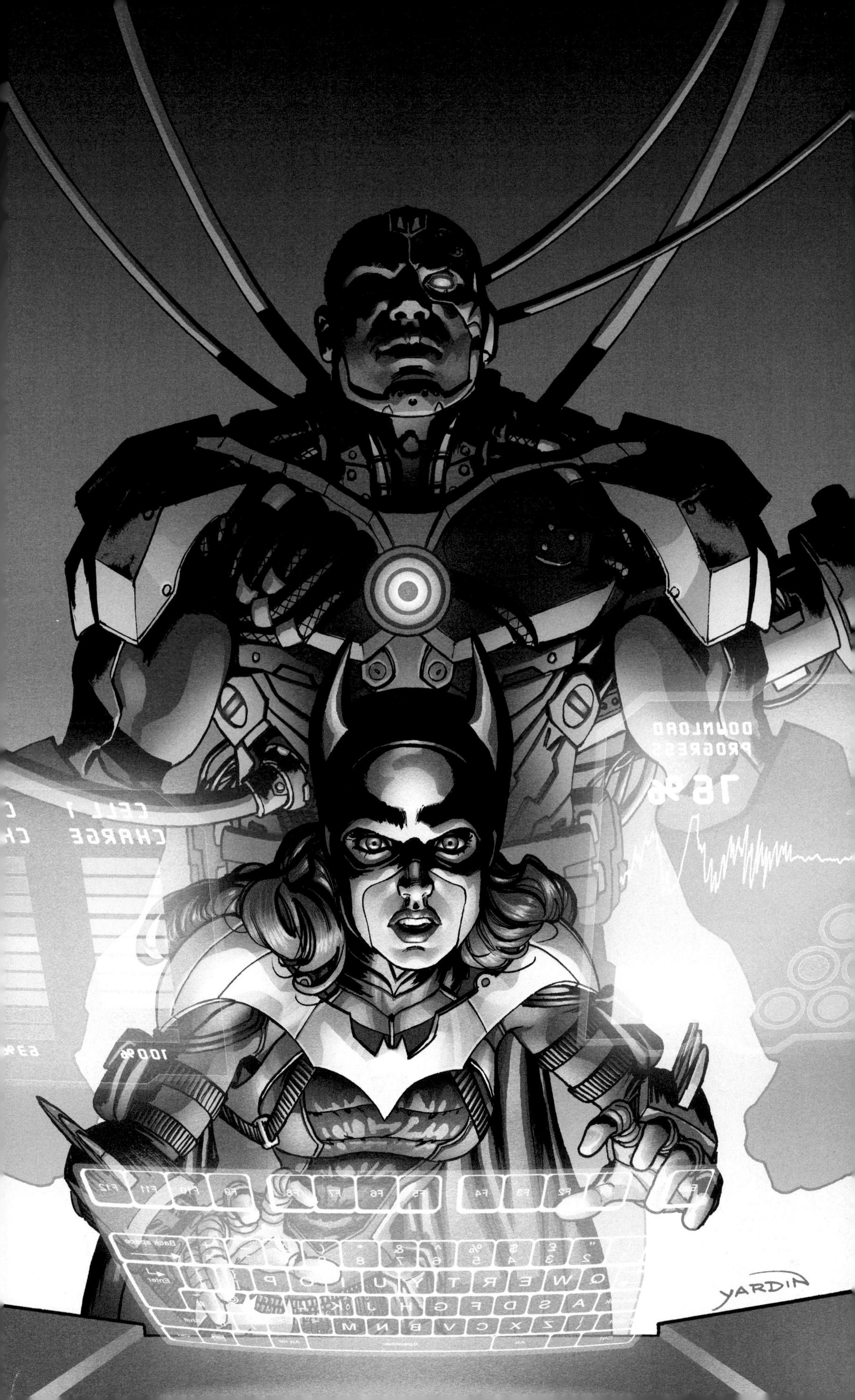

CELL 1
CHARGE
100%
DOWNLOAD
PROGRESS
18%
YARDIN

"Surgical Strike" Marco Santucci Artist Rex Lokus Colorist

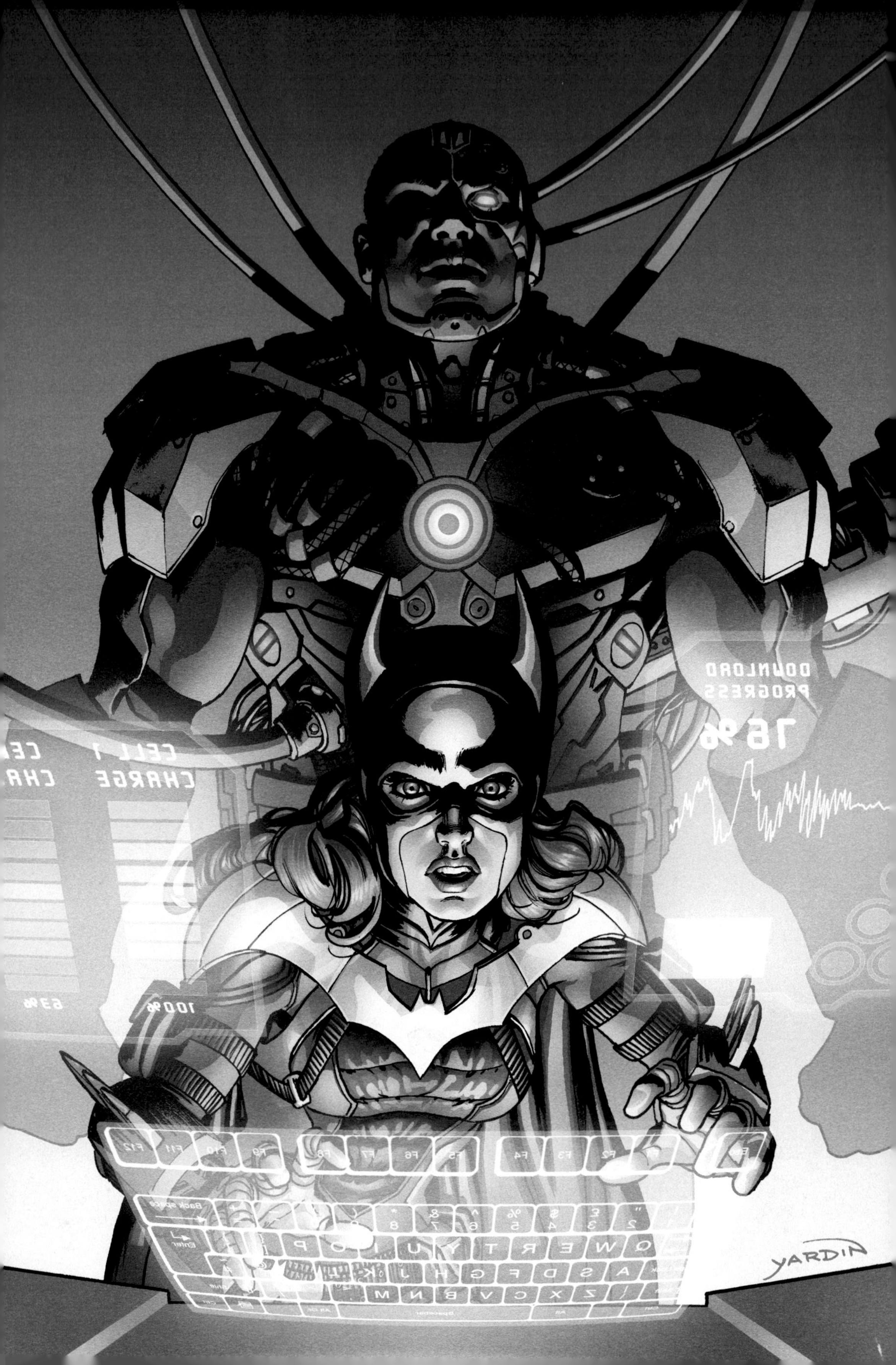

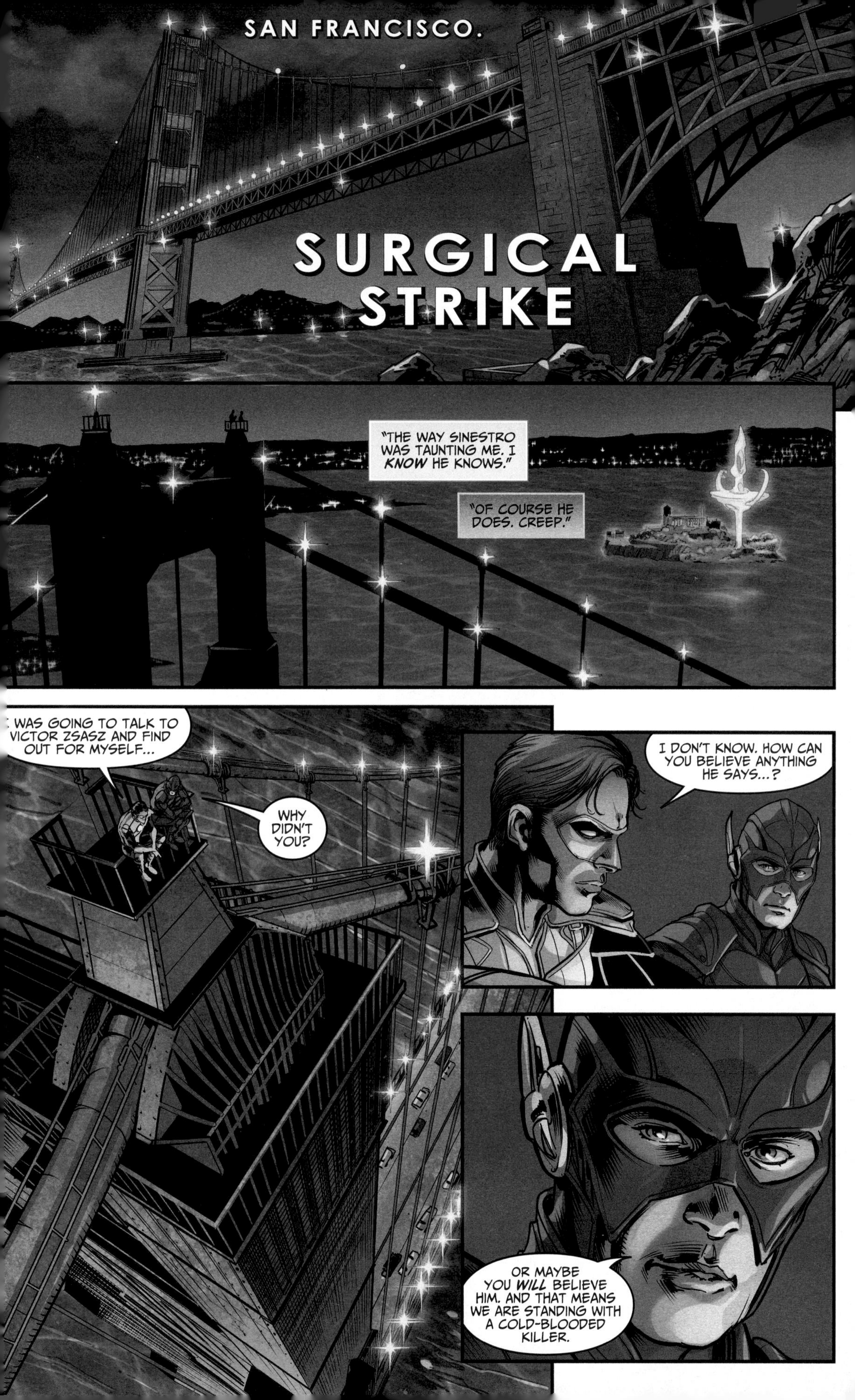

SAN FRANCISCO.
SURGICAL STRIKE
"THE WAY SINESTRO WAS TAUNTING ME. I *KNOW* HE KNOWS."
"OF COURSE HE DOES. CREEP."
I WAS GOING TO TALK TO VICTOR ZSASZ AND FIND OUT FOR MYSELF...
WHY DIDN'T YOU?
I DON'T KNOW. HOW CAN YOU BELIEVE ANYTHING HE SAYS...?
OR MAYBE YOU *WILL* BELIEVE HIM. AND THAT MEANS WE ARE STANDING WITH A COLD-BLOODED KILLER.

WASHINGTON DC.

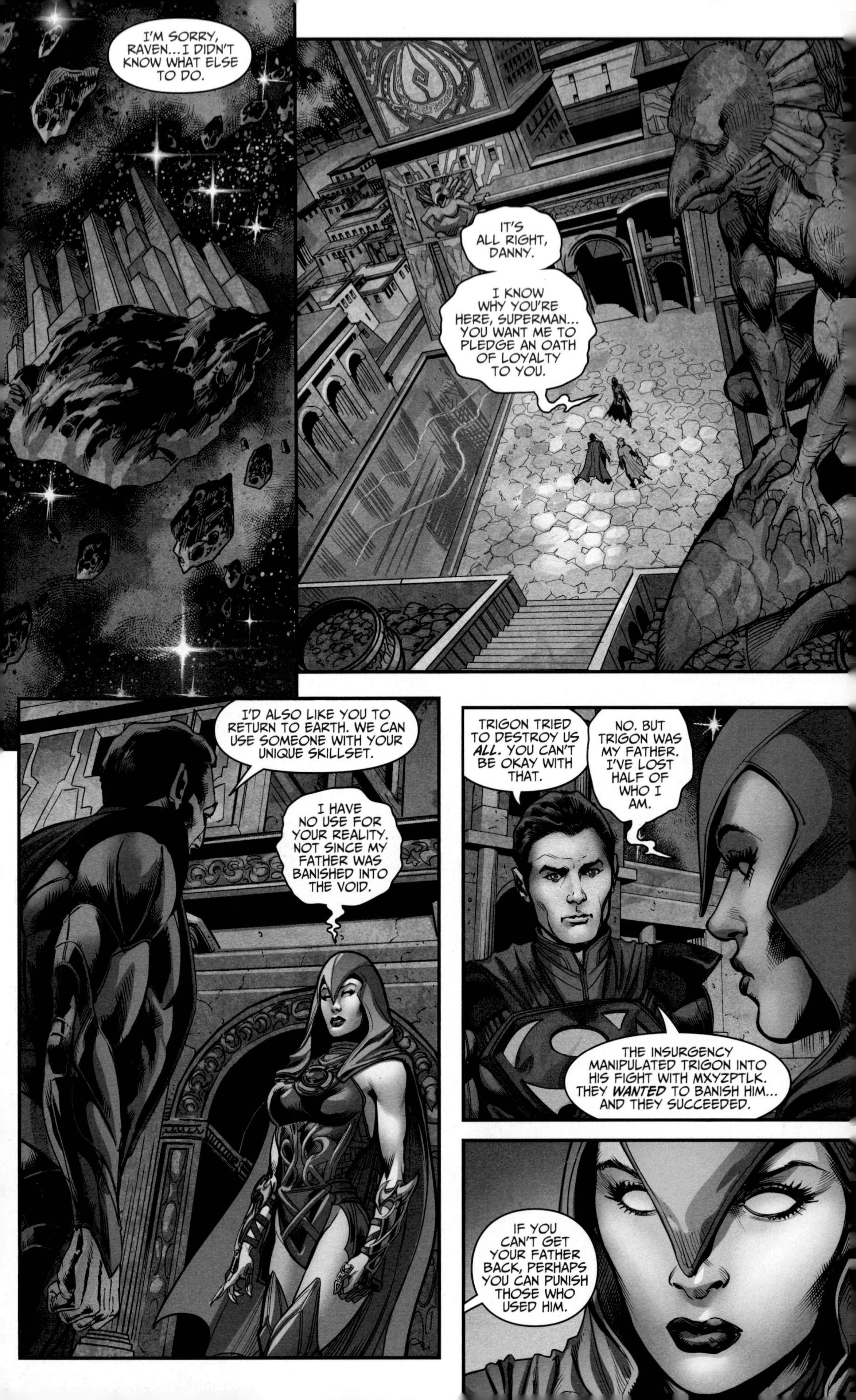
I'M SORRY, RAVEN... I DIDN'T KNOW WHAT ELSE TO DO.
IT'S ALL RIGHT, DANNY.
I KNOW WHY YOU'RE HERE, SUPERMAN... YOU WANT ME TO PLEDGE AN OATH OF LOYALTY TO YOU.
I'D ALSO LIKE YOU TO RETURN TO EARTH. WE CAN USE SOMEONE WITH YOUR UNIQUE SKILLSET.
I HAVE NO USE FOR YOUR REALITY. NOT SINCE MY FATHER WAS BANISHED INTO THE VOID.
TRIGON TRIED TO DESTROY US ALL. YOU CAN'T BE OKAY WITH THAT.
NO. BUT TRIGON WAS MY FATHER. I'VE LOST HALF OF WHO I AM.
THE INSURGENCY MANIPULATED TRIGON INTO HIS FIGHT WITH MXYZPTLK. THEY WANTED TO BANISH HIM... AND THEY SUCCEEDED.
IF YOU CAN'T GET YOUR FATHER BACK, PERHAPS YOU CAN PUNISH THOSE WHO USED HIM.

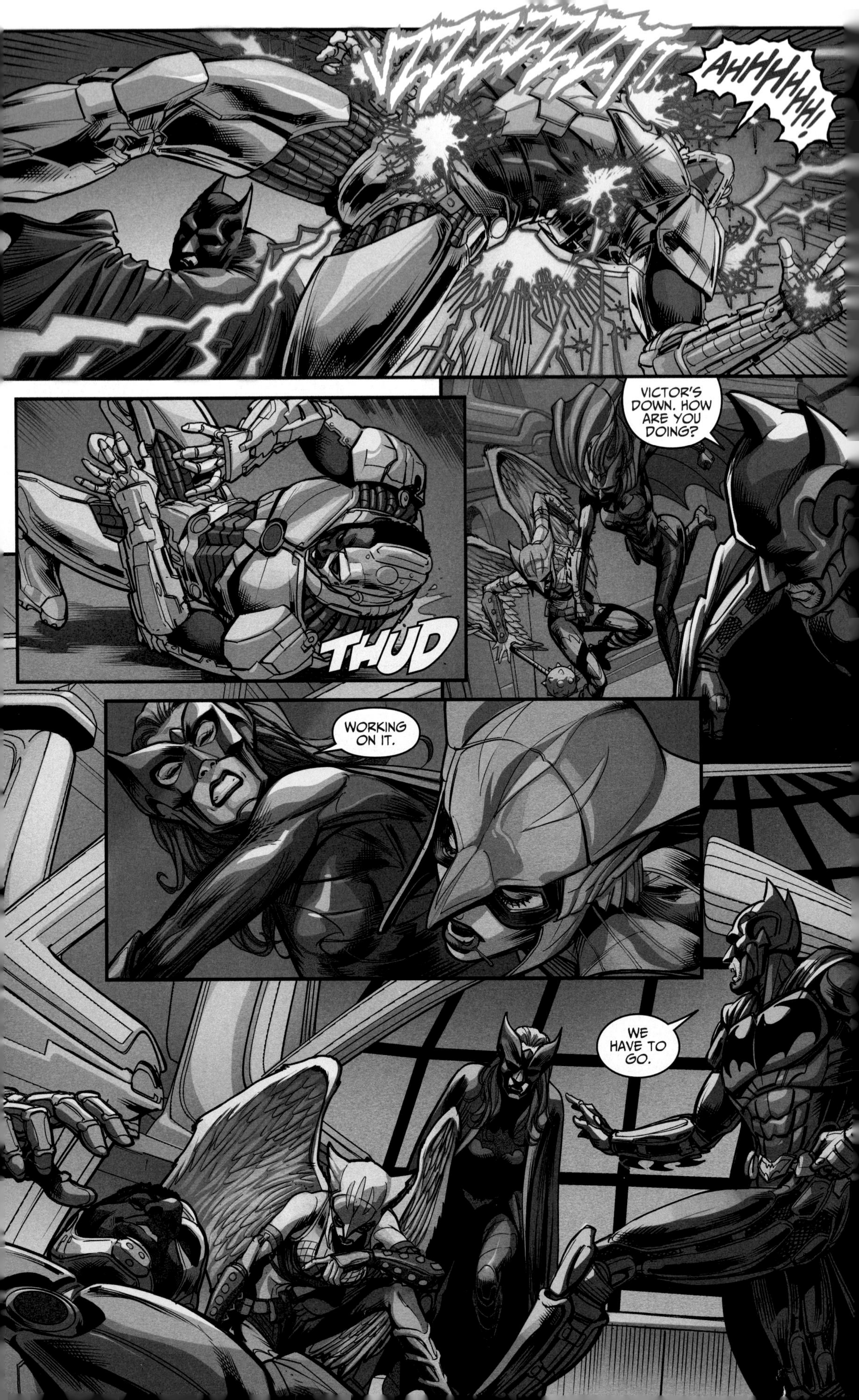
AHHHHH!
THUD
VICTOR'S DOWN. HOW ARE YOU DOING?
WORKING ON IT.
WE HAVE TO GO.

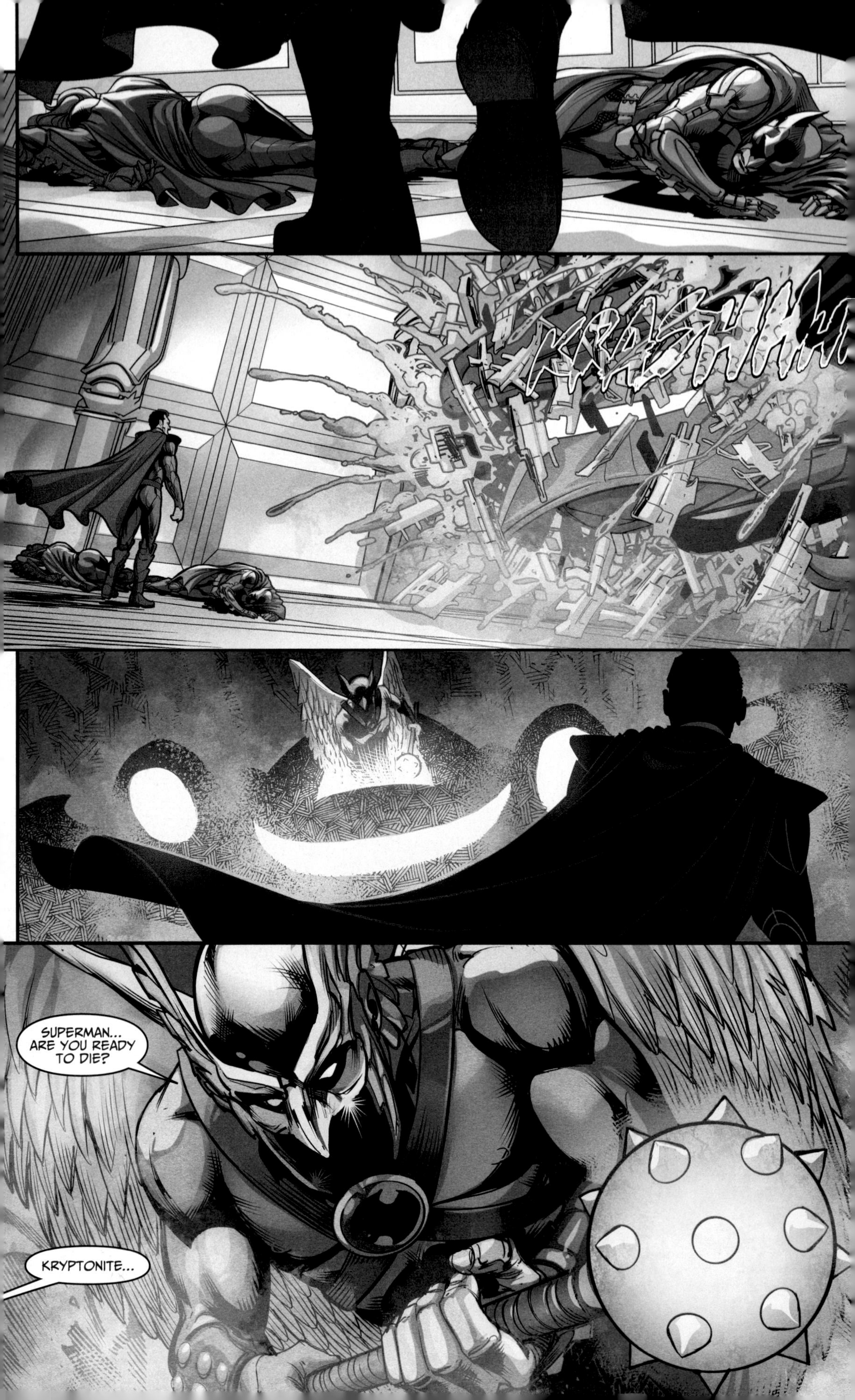
KRASHHH
SUPERMAN... ARE YOU READY TO DIE?
KRYPTONITE...

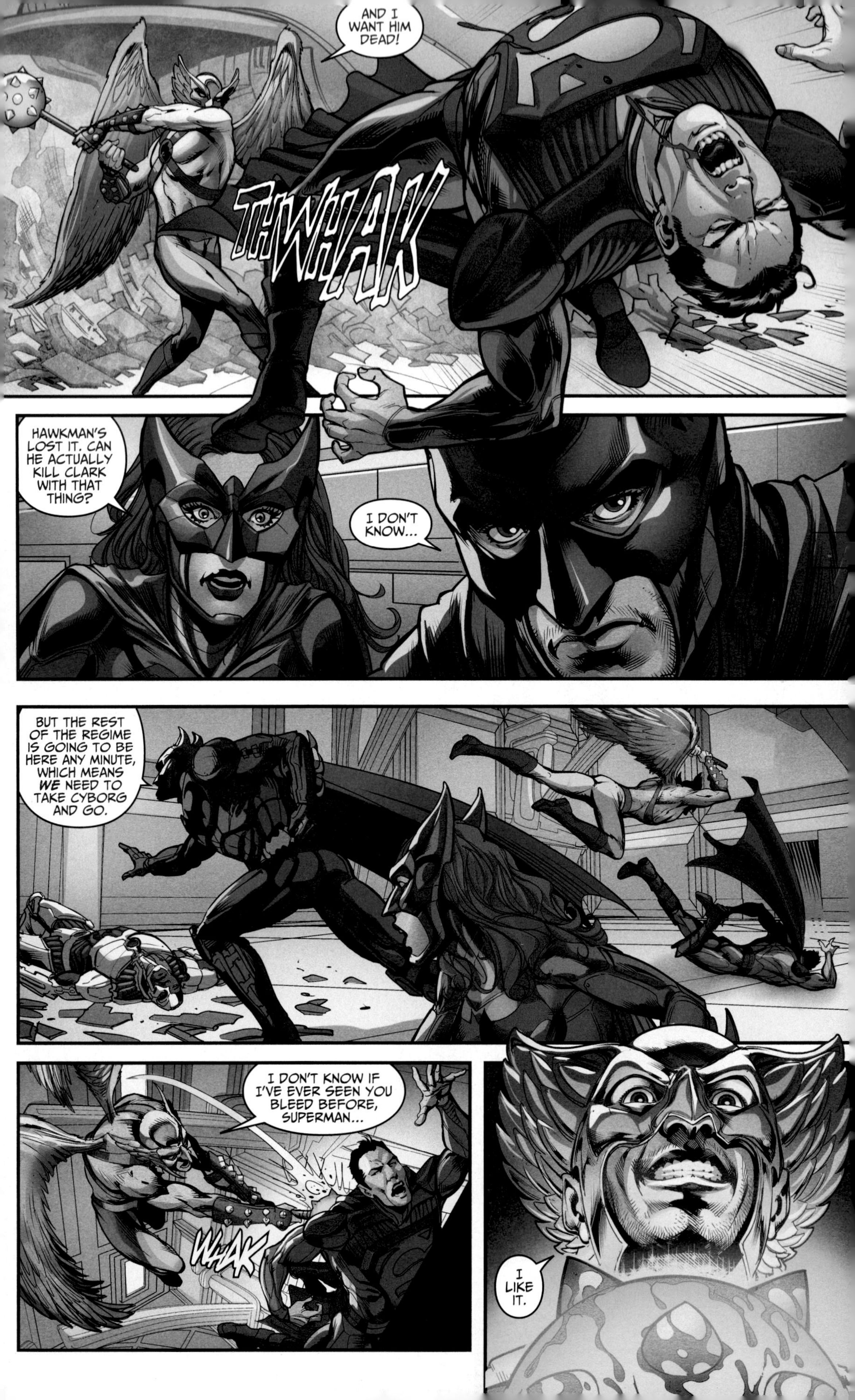
AND I WANT HIM DEAD!
THWHAK
HAWKMAN'S LOST IT. CAN HE ACTUALLY KILL CLARK WITH THAT THING?
I DON'T KNOW...
BUT THE REST OF THE REGIME IS GOING TO BE HERE ANY MINUTE, WHICH MEANS *WE* NEED TO TAKE CYBORG AND GO.
I DON'T KNOW IF I'VE EVER SEEN YOU BLEED BEFORE, SUPERMAN...
WHAK
I LIKE IT.

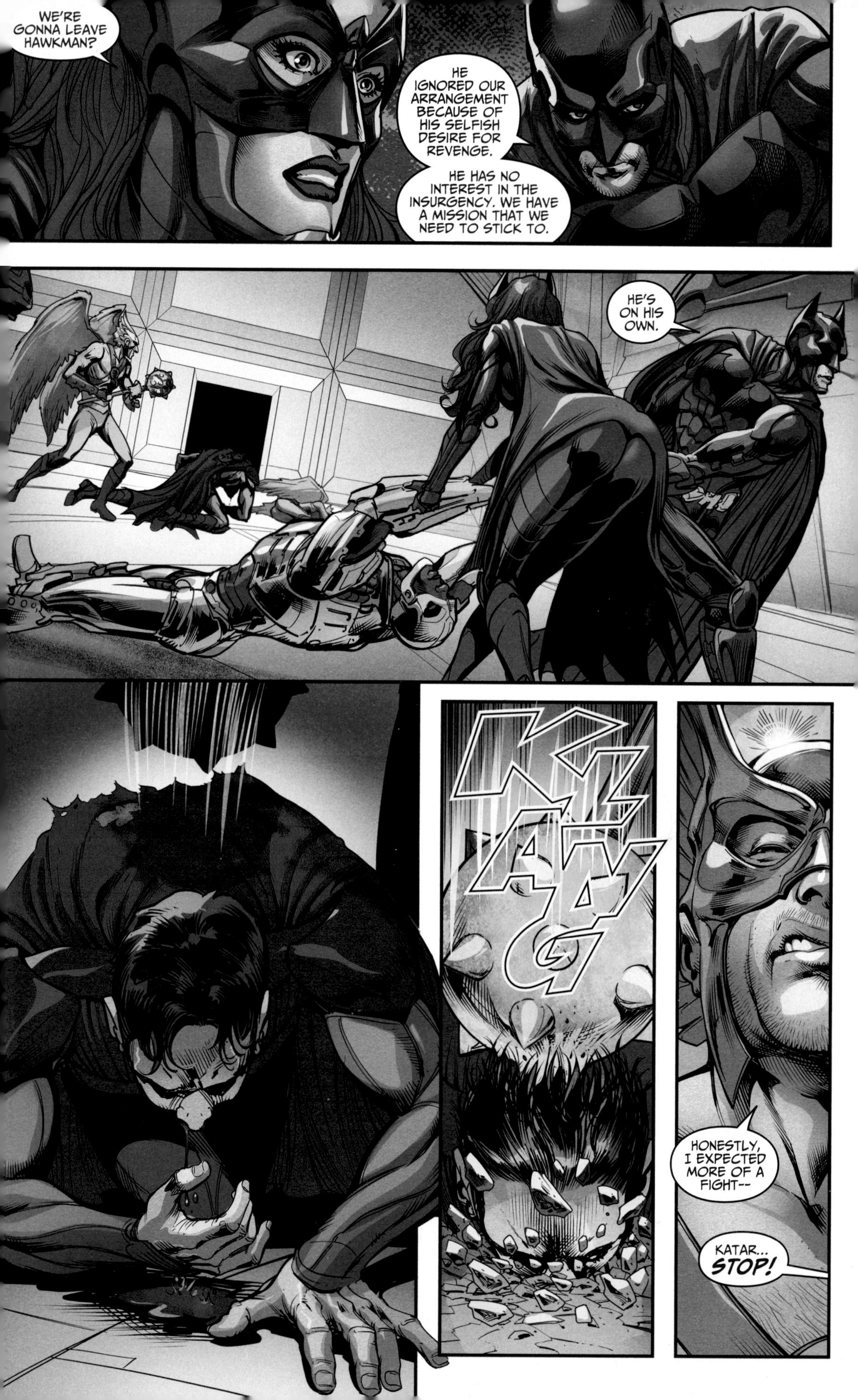
WE'RE GONNA LEAVE HAWKMAN?
HE IGNORED OUR ARRANGEMENT BECAUSE OF HIS SELFISH DESIRE FOR REVENGE.
HE HAS NO INTEREST IN THE INSURGENCY. WE HAVE A MISSION THAT WE NEED TO STICK TO.
HE'S ON HIS OWN.
KLANG
HONESTLY, I EXPECTED MORE OF A FIGHT--
KATAR... STOP!

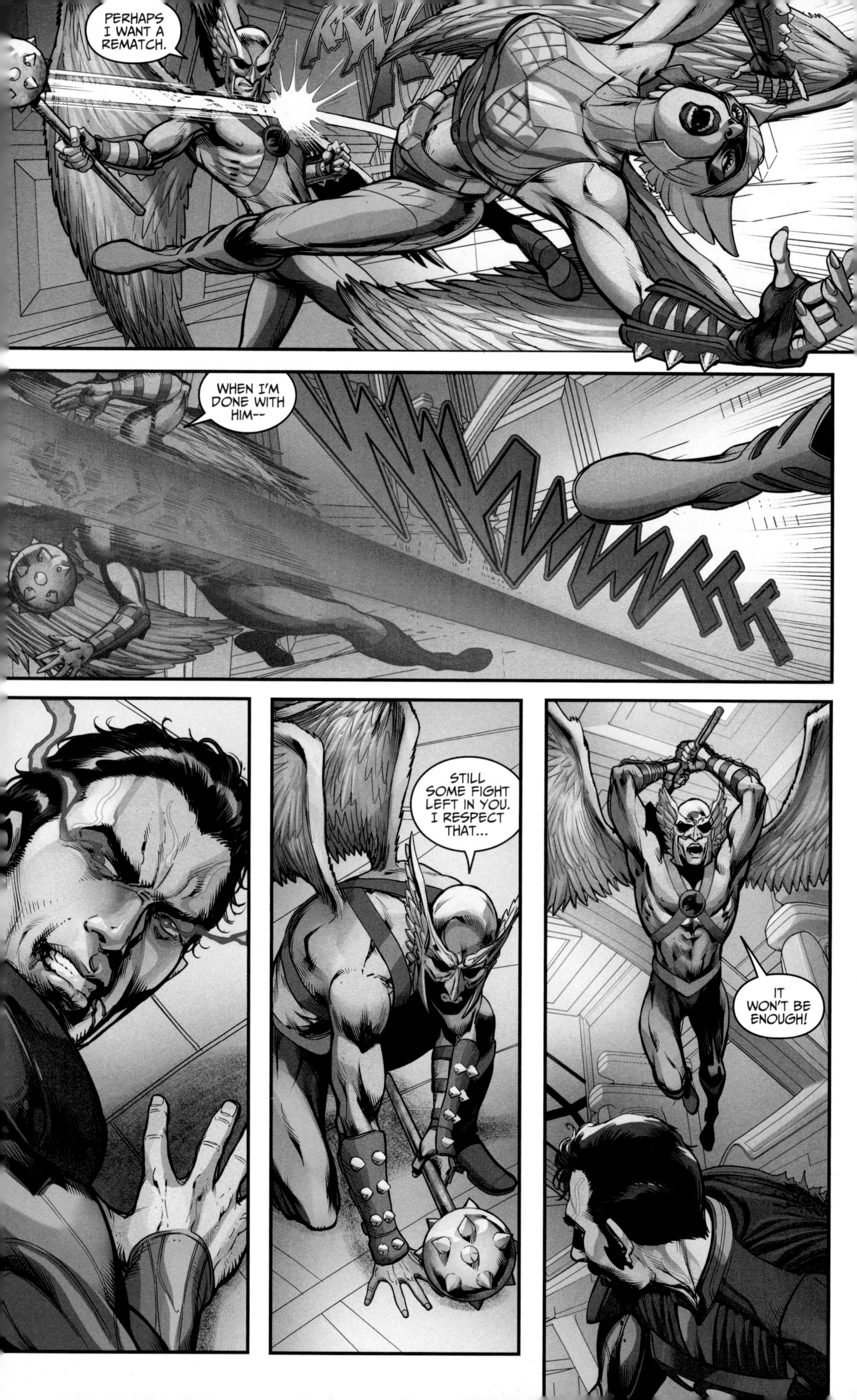
PERHAPS I WANT A REMATCH.
KRAK
WHEN I'M DONE WITH HIM--
STILL SOME FIGHT LEFT IN YOU. I RESPECT THAT...
IT WON'T BE ENOUGH!

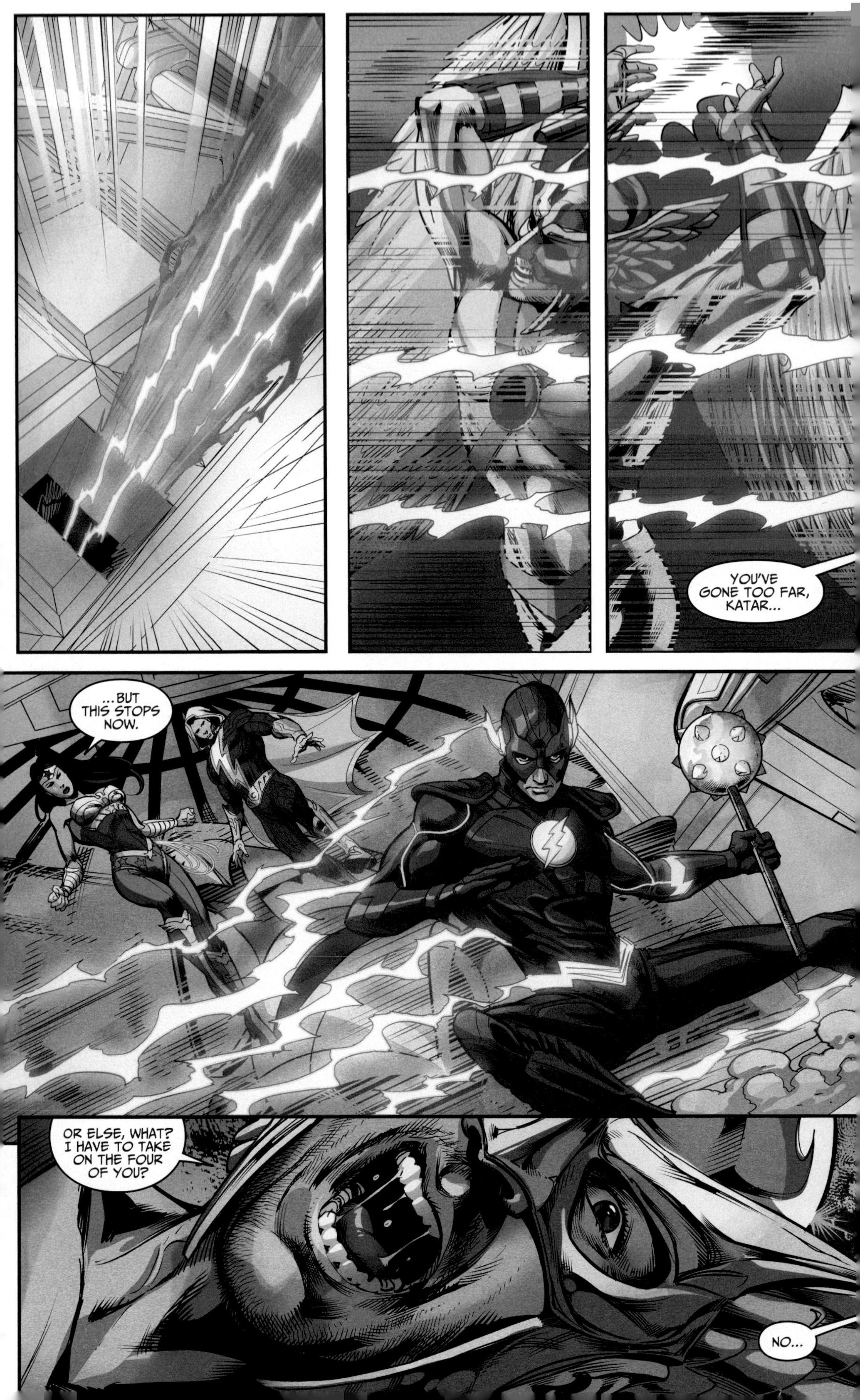
YOU'VE GONE TOO FAR, KATAR...
...BUT THIS STOPS NOW.
OR ELSE, WHAT? I HAVE TO TAKE ON THE FOUR OF YOU?
NO...

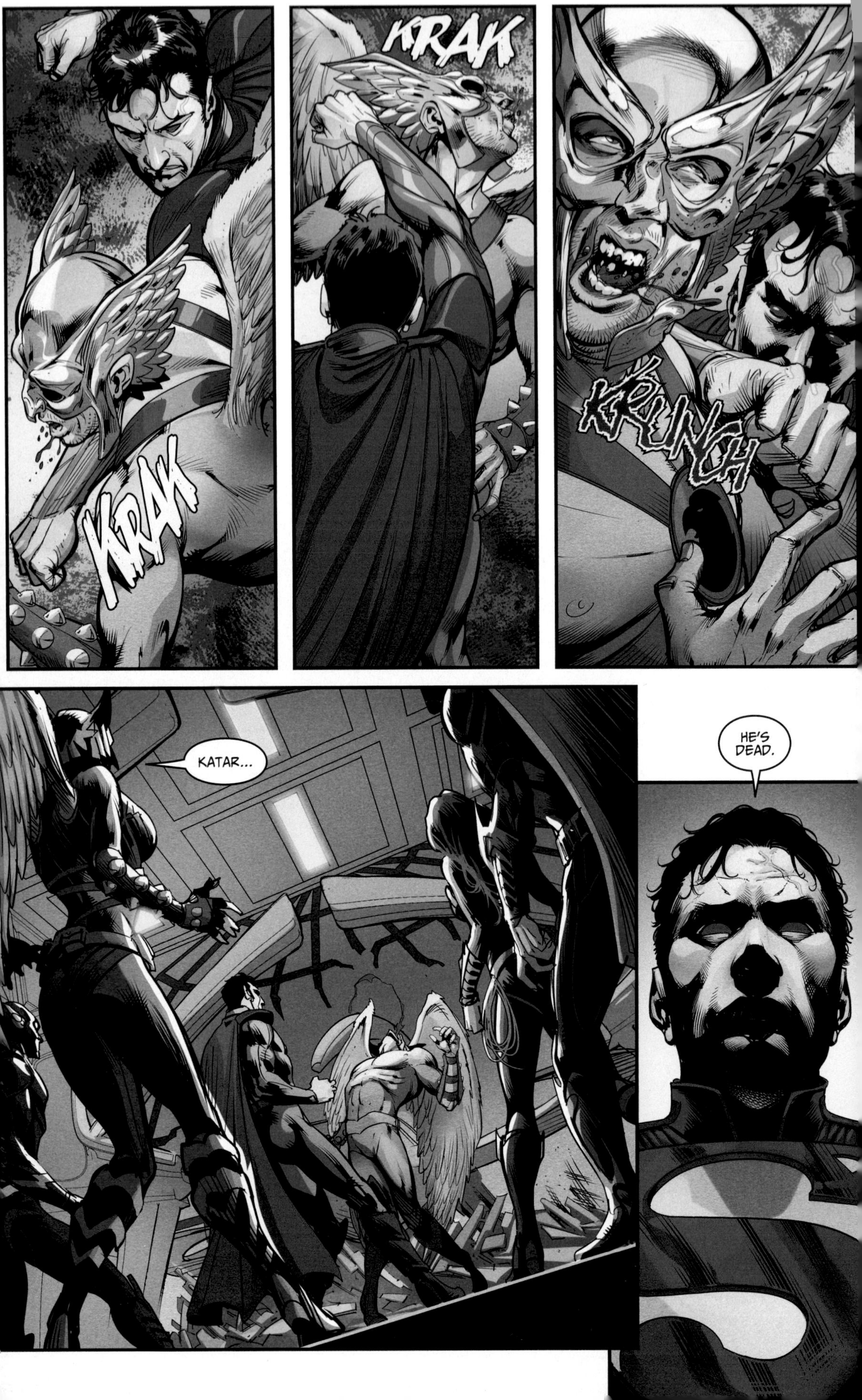
KRAK
KRAK
KRUNCH
KATAR...
HE'S DEAD.

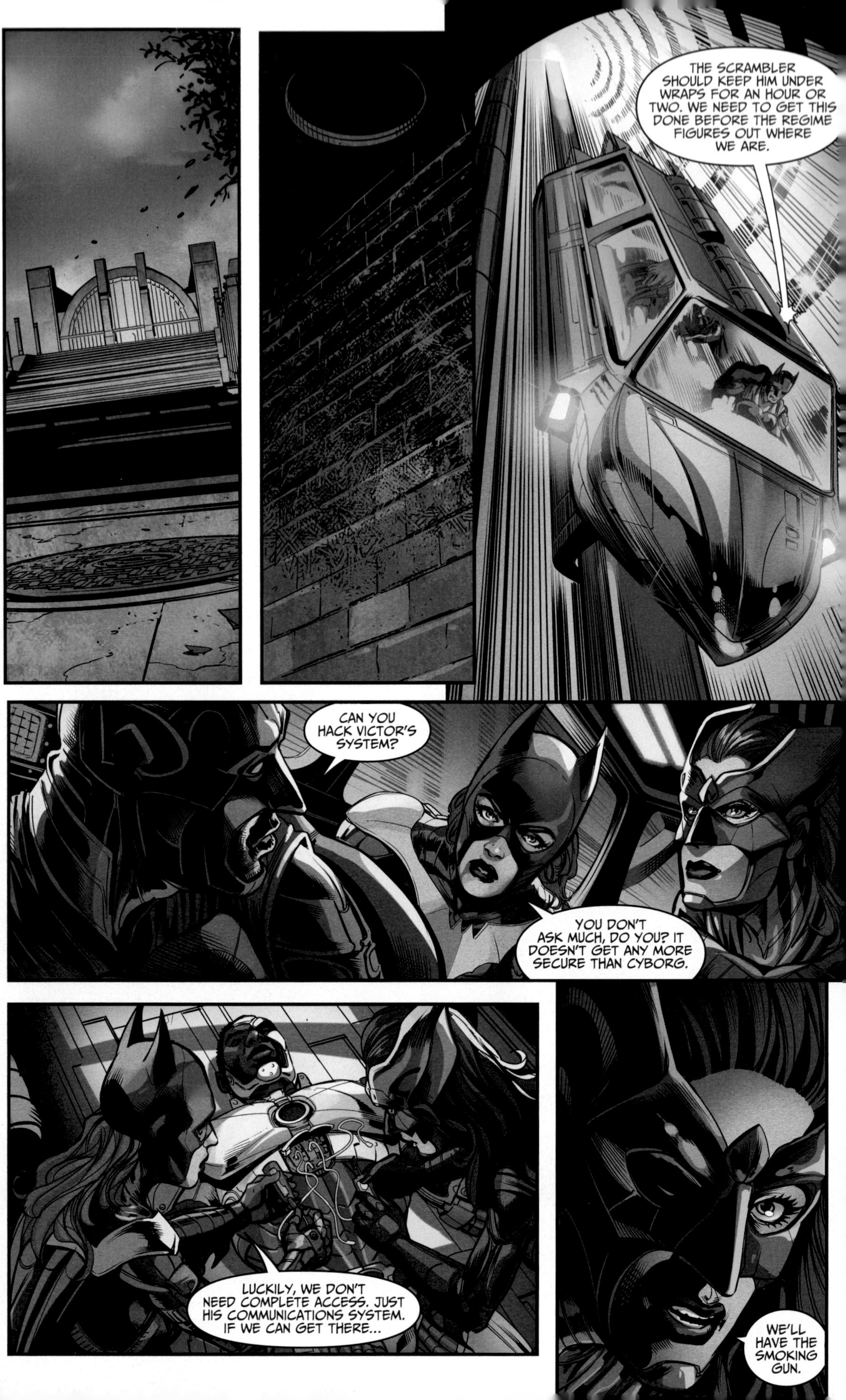
THE SCRAMBLER SHOULD KEEP HIM UNDER WRAPS FOR AN HOUR OR TWO. WE NEED TO GET THIS DONE BEFORE THE REGIME FIGURES OUT WHERE WE ARE.
CAN YOU HACK VICTOR'S SYSTEM?
YOU DON'T ASK MUCH, DO YOU? IT DOESN'T GET ANY MORE SECURE THAN CYBORG.
LUCKILY, WE DON'T NEED COMPLETE ACCESS. JUST HIS COMMUNICATIONS SYSTEM. IF WE CAN GET THERE...
WE'LL HAVE THE SMOKING GUN.

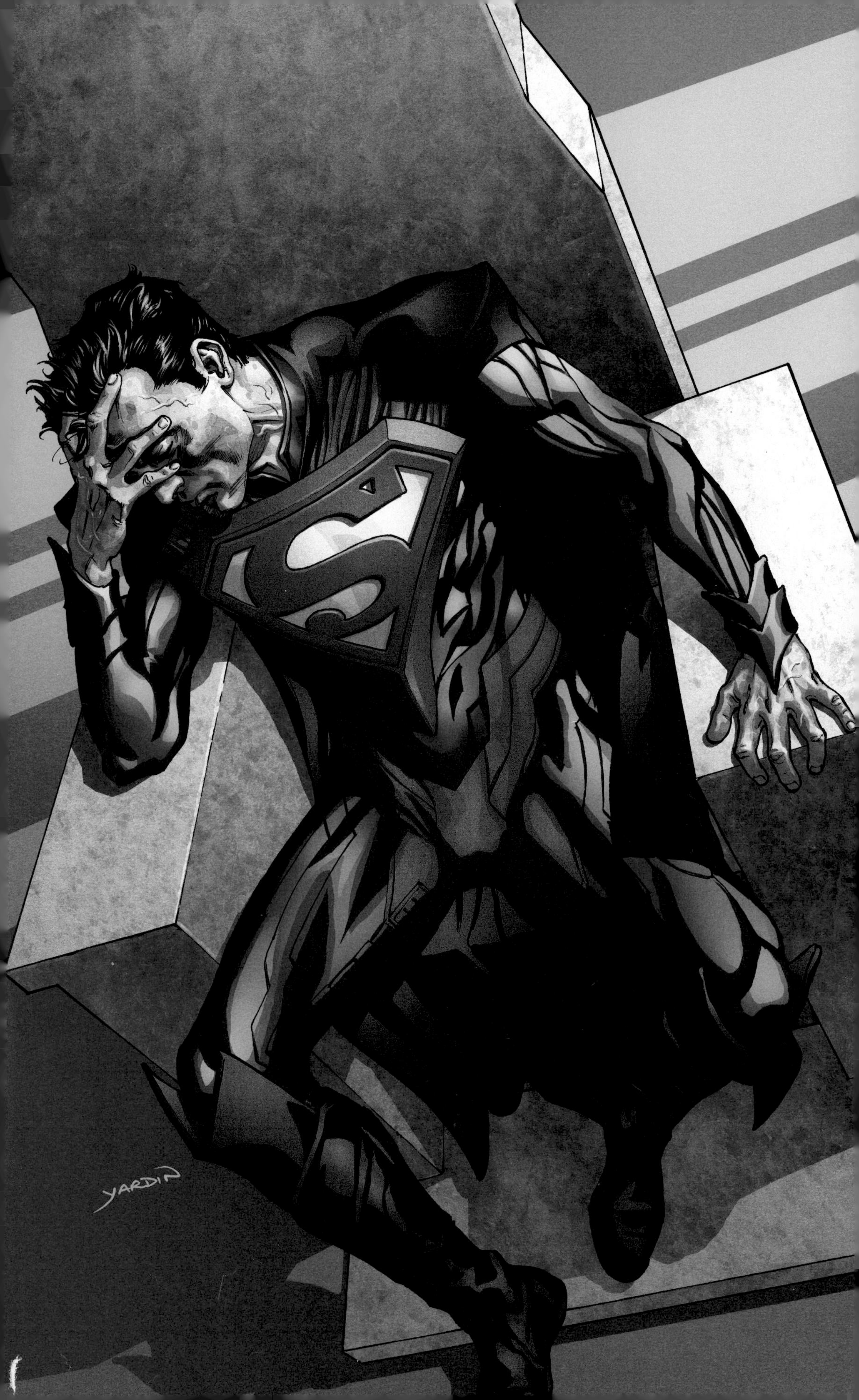
YARDIN

"The Smoking Gun" **Tom Derenick** Artist **Rex Lokus** Colorist

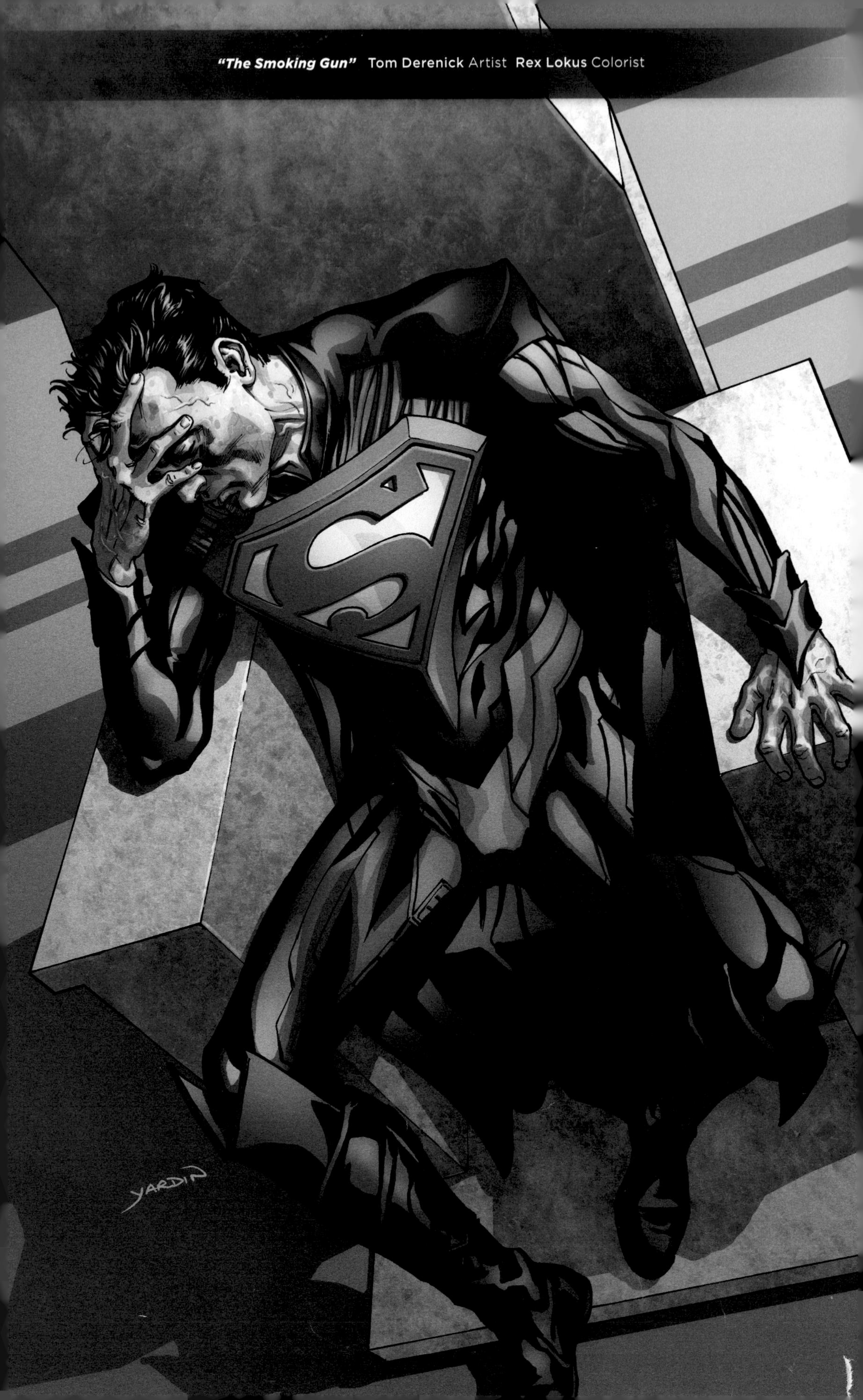
YARDIN

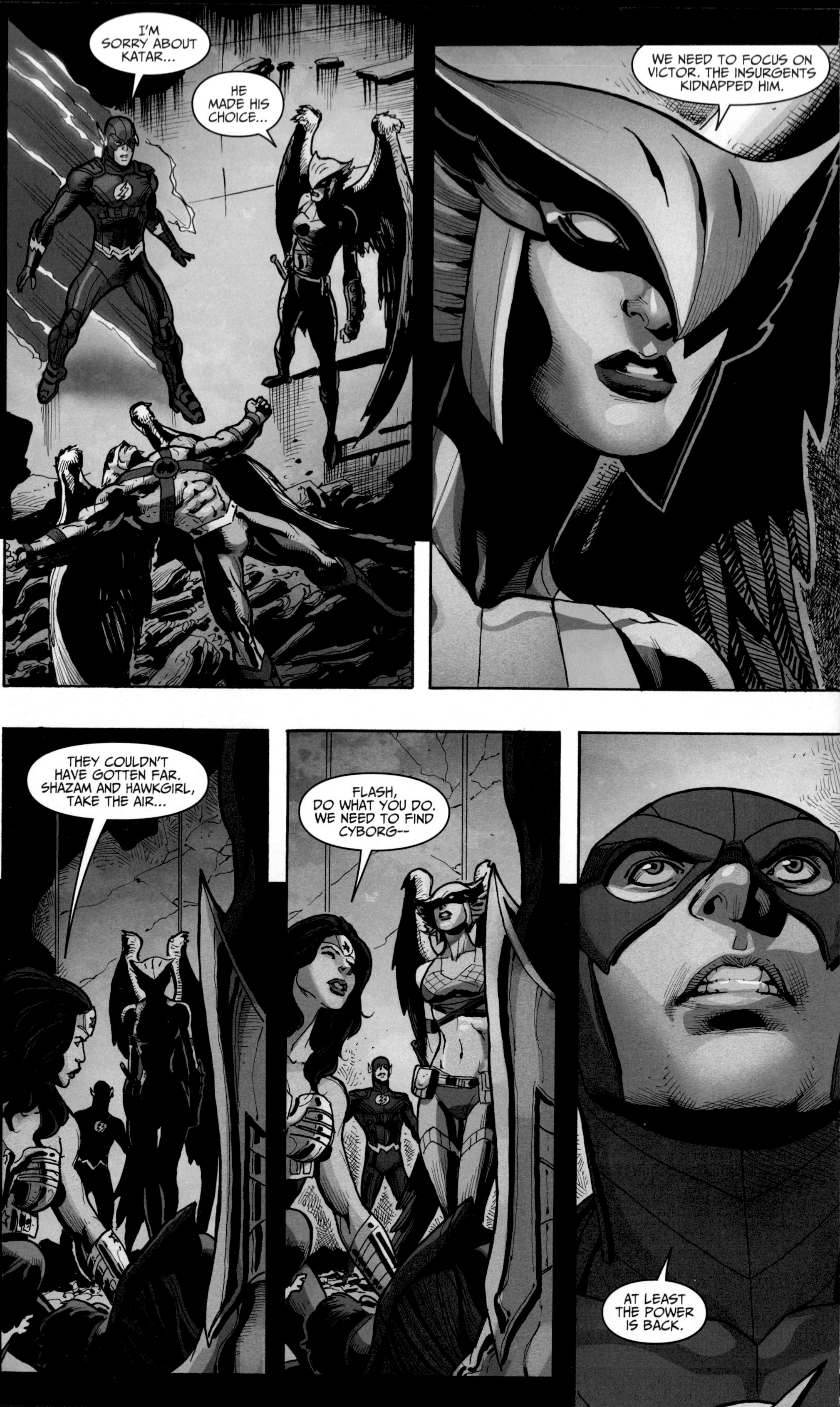
I'M SORRY ABOUT KATAR...
HE MADE HIS CHOICE...
WE NEED TO FOCUS ON VICTOR. THE INSURGENTS KIDNAPPED HIM.
THEY COULDN'T HAVE GOTTEN FAR. SHAZAM AND HAWKGIRL, TAKE THE AIR...
FLASH, DO WHAT YOU DO. WE NEED TO FIND CYBORG--
AT LEAST THE POWER IS BACK.

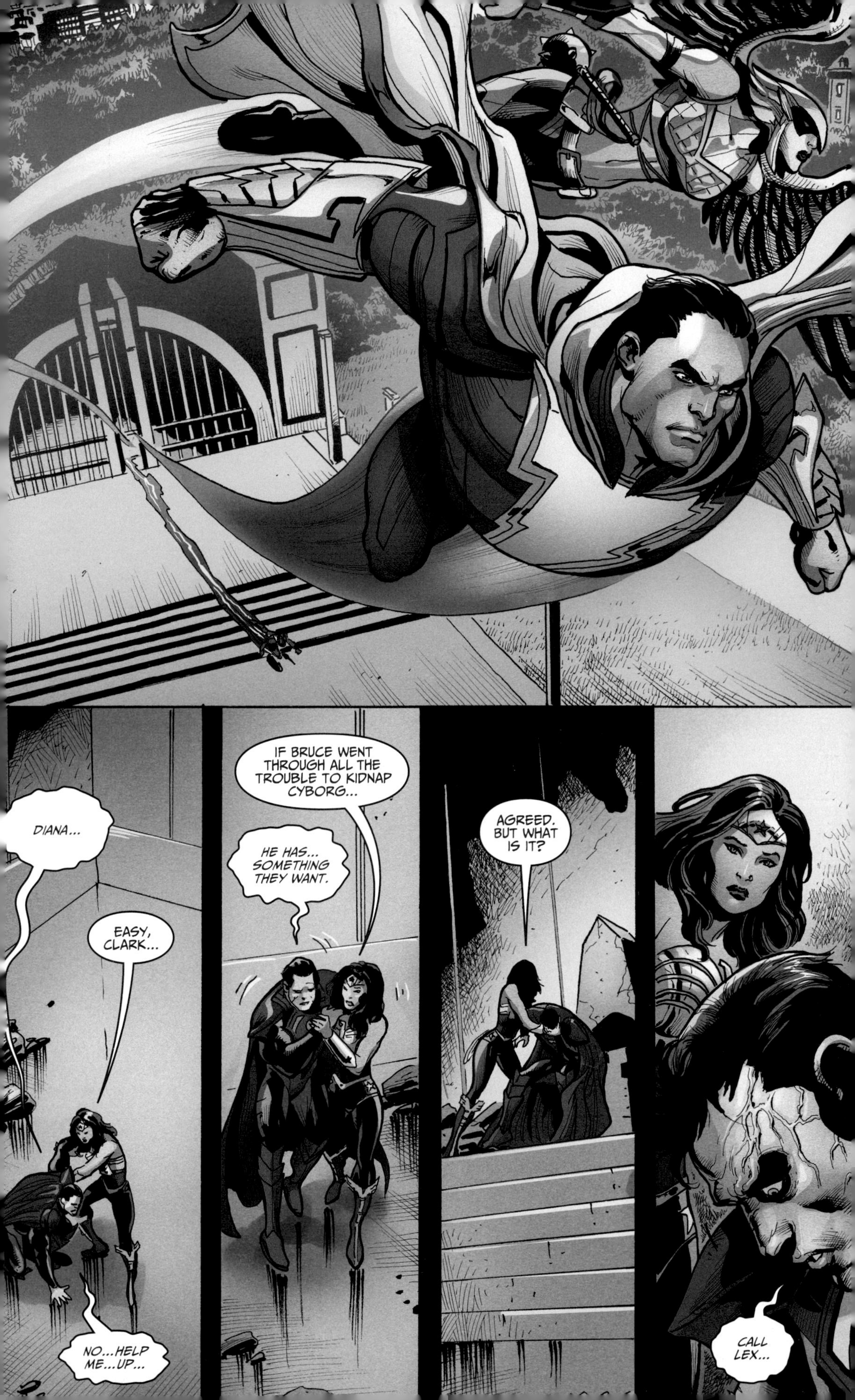
DIANA...
EASY, CLARK...
NO...HELP ME...UP...
IF BRUCE WENT THROUGH ALL THE TROUBLE TO KIDNAP CYBORG...
HE HAS... SOMETHING THEY WANT.
AGREED. BUT WHAT IS IT?
CALL LEX...

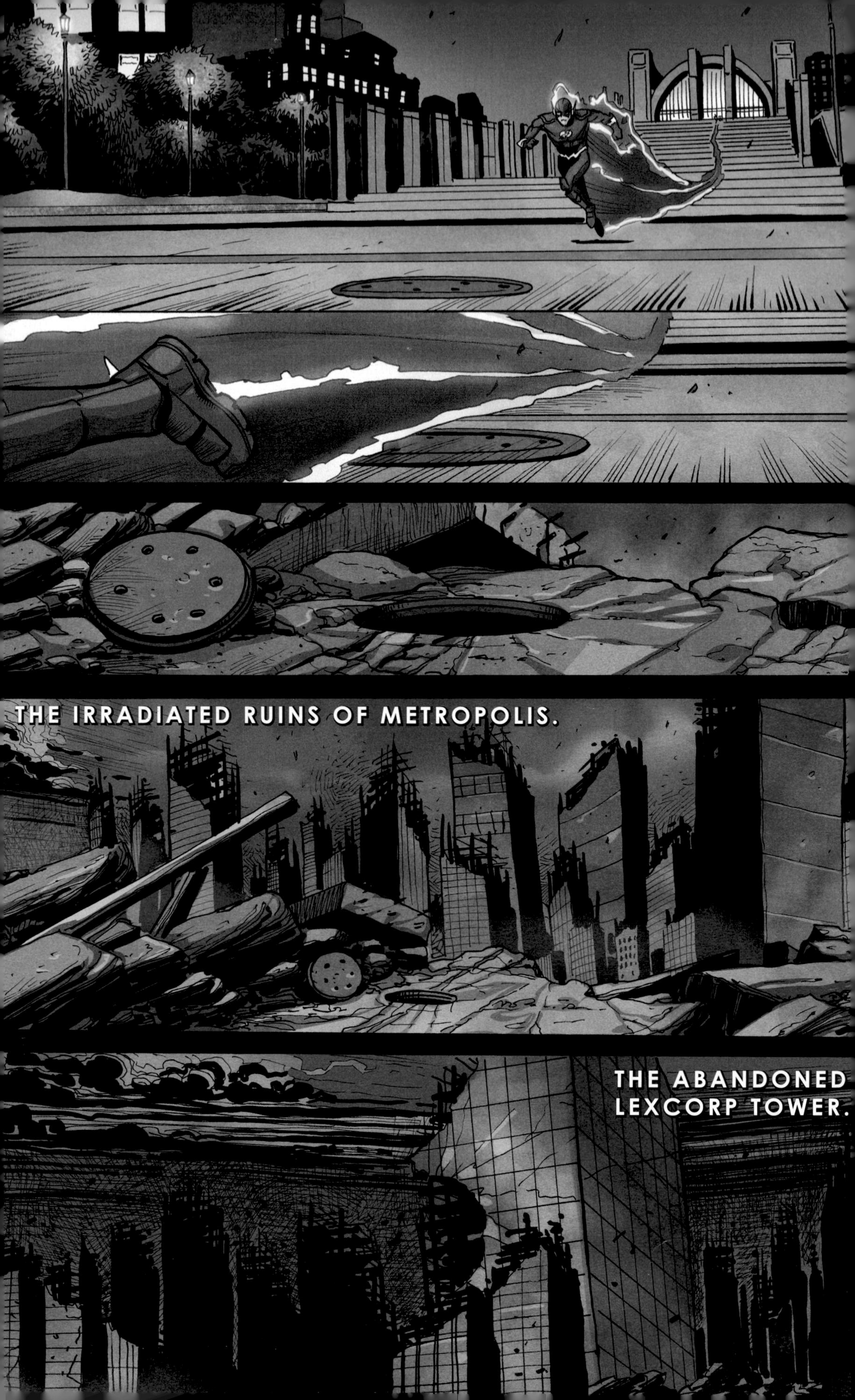
THE IRRADIATED RUINS OF METROPOLIS.
THE ABANDONED LEXCORP TOWER.

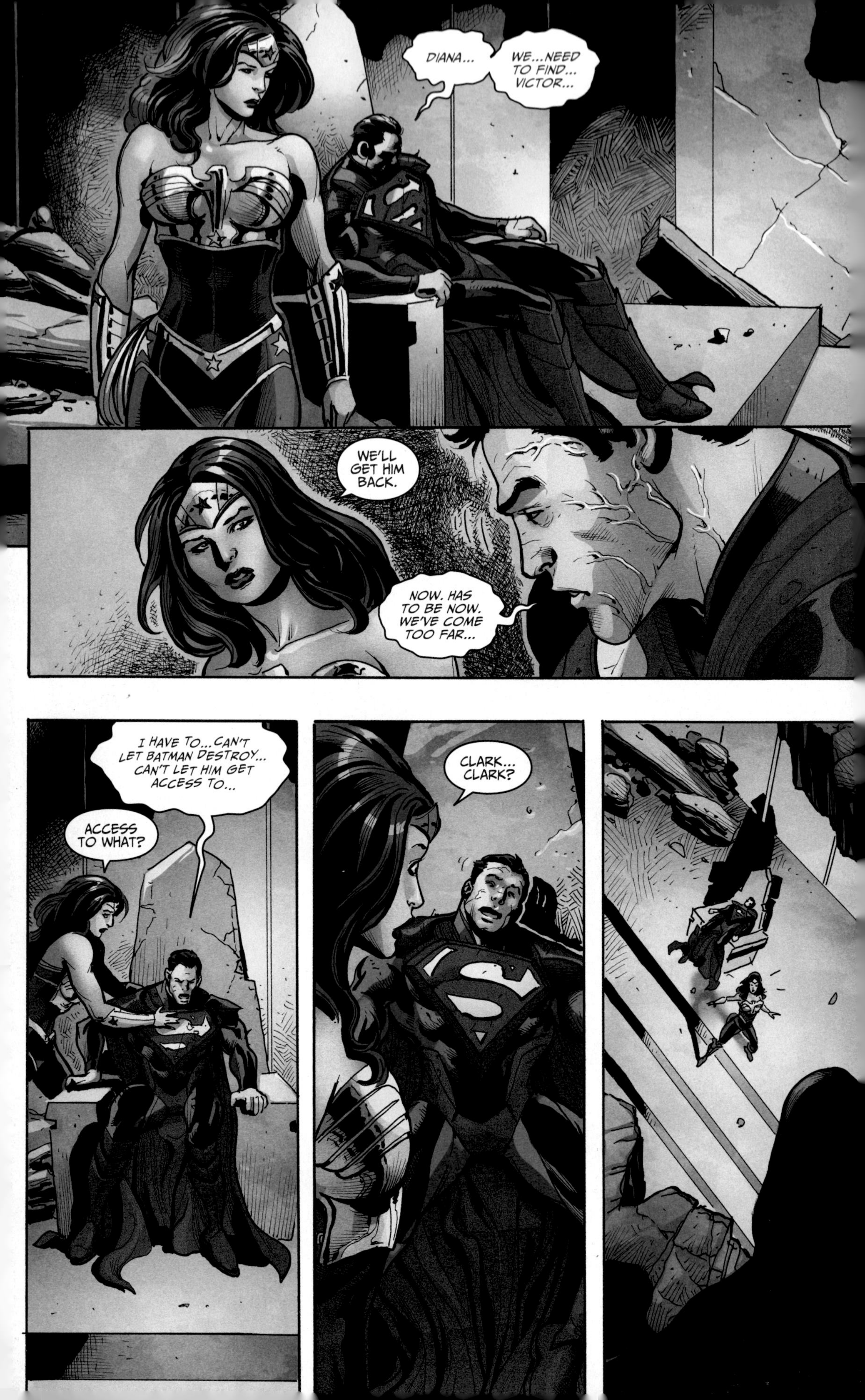
DIANA...
WE...NEED TO FIND... VICTOR...
WE'LL GET HIM BACK.
NOW. HAS TO BE NOW. WE'VE COME TOO FAR...
I HAVE TO...CAN'T LET BATMAN DESTROY... CAN'T LET HIM GET ACCESS TO...
ACCESS TO WHAT?
CLARK... CLARK?

"I HAVE ALL OF MY SATELLITES SEARCHING FOR HIM...

...BUT I'M COMING UP EMPTY. WHEREVER THEY TOOK CYBORG... HE'S OFF THE GRID.

THAT'S A PROBLEM. WE DON'T EVEN KNOW WHERE TO LOOK.

YEAH. I'M FAST, BUT EVEN I CAN'T CHECK EVERY PLACE ON EARTH.

WELL, HE DIDN'T JUST VANISH. KEEP LOOKING.

AND LEX... I NEED YOU HERE AS SOON AS YOU CAN. CLARK'S IN BAD SHAPE.

LET ME GRAB SOME EQUIPMENT AND I'LL HEAD OVER.

VZZT

VZZZZT

SORRY TO INTRUDE. I NEED A WORD...

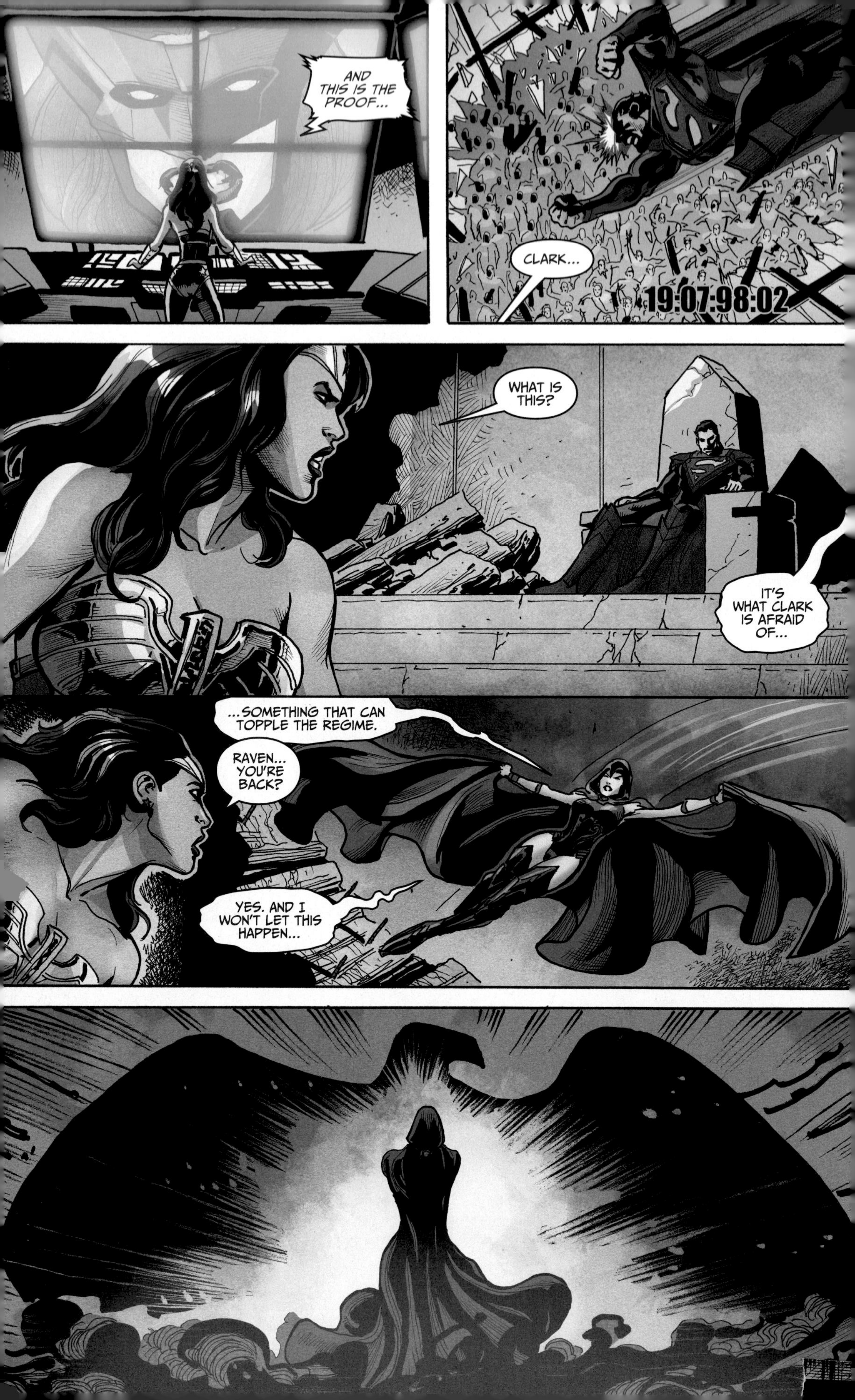
AND THIS IS THE PROOF...
CLARK...
19:07:98:02
WHAT IS THIS?
IT'S WHAT CLARK IS AFRAID OF...
...SOMETHING THAT CAN TOPPLE THE REGIME.
RAVEN... YOU'RE BACK?
YES. AND I WON'T LET THIS HAPPEN...

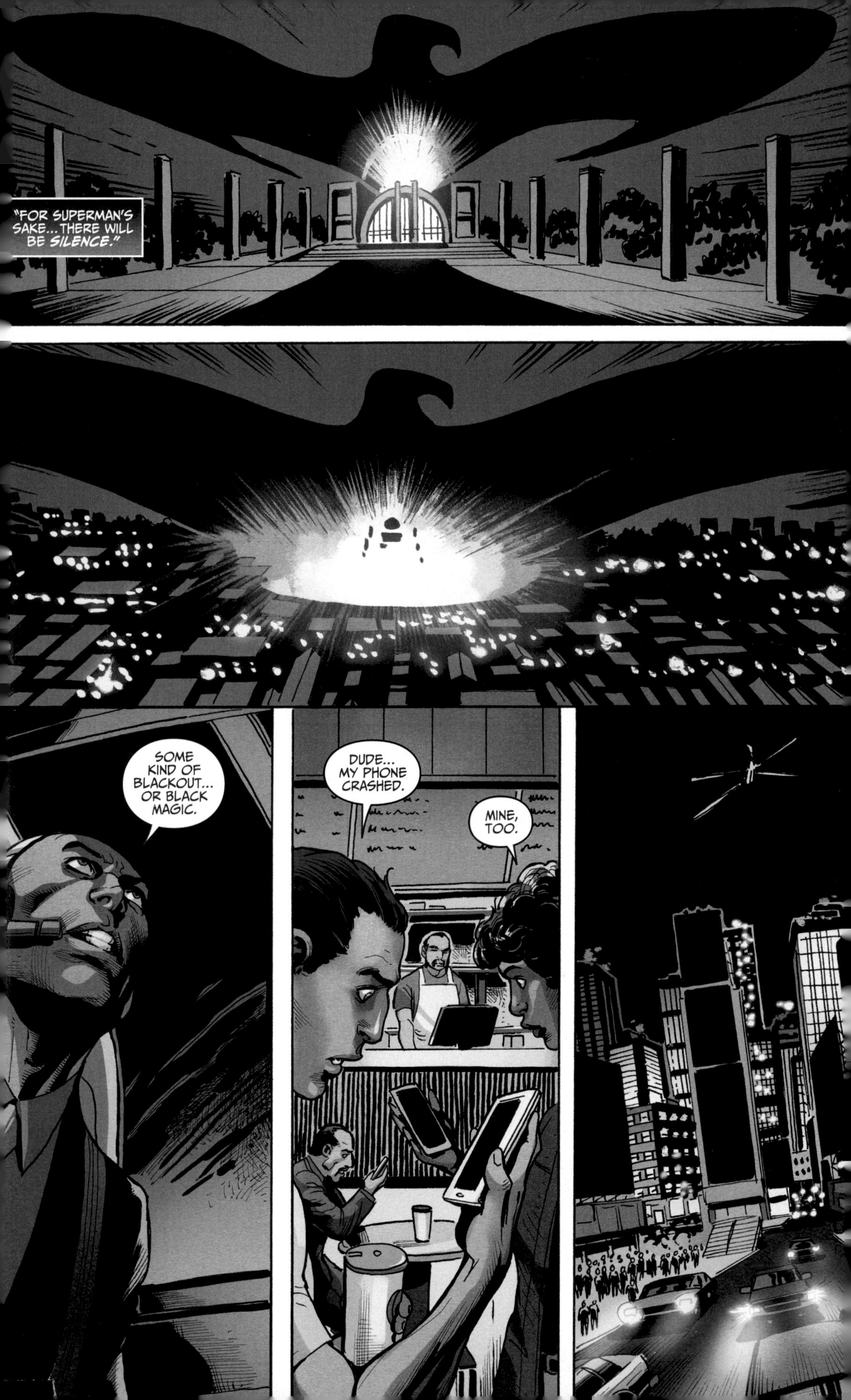
"FOR SUPERMAN'S SAKE... THERE WILL BE SILENCE."
SOME KIND OF BLACKOUT... OR BLACK MAGIC.
DUDE... MY PHONE CRASHED.
MINE, TOO.

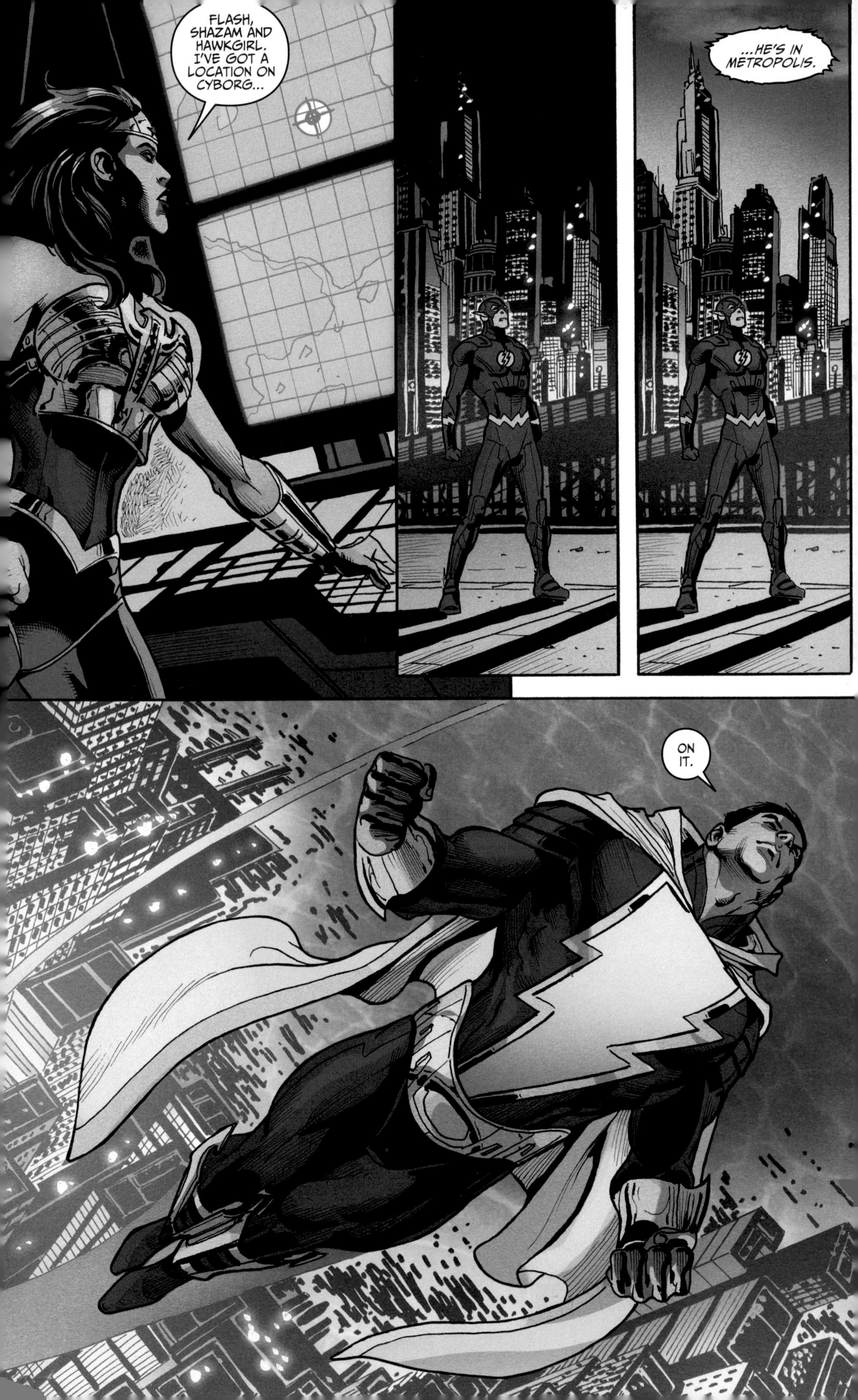
FLASH, SHAZAM AND HAWKGIRL. I'VE GOT A LOCATION ON CYBORG...
...HE'S IN METROPOLIS.
ON IT.

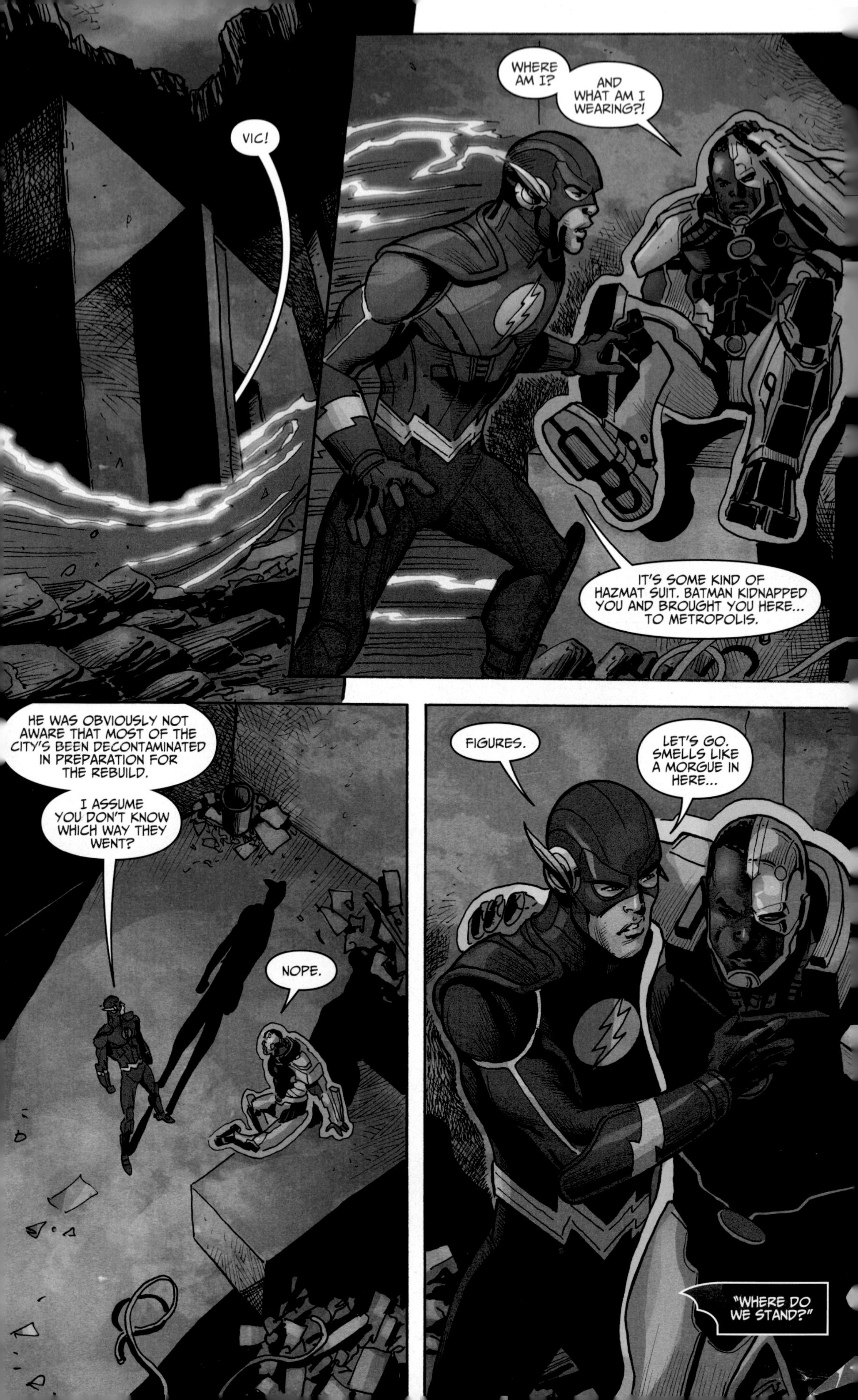
VIC!
WHERE AM I?
AND WHAT AM I WEARING?!
IT'S SOME KIND OF HAZMAT SUIT. BATMAN KIDNAPPED YOU AND BROUGHT YOU HERE... TO METROPOLIS.
HE WAS OBVIOUSLY NOT AWARE THAT MOST OF THE CITY'S BEEN DECONTAMINATED IN PREPARATION FOR THE REBUILD.
I ASSUME YOU DON'T KNOW WHICH WAY THEY WENT?
NOPE.
FIGURES.
LET'S GO. SMELLS LIKE A MORGUE IN HERE...
"WHERE DO WE STAND?"

"YOU'RE GOING TO BE FINE, CLARK..."

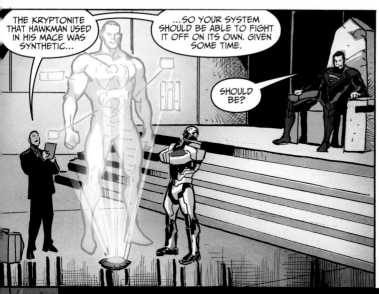

THE KRYPTONITE THAT HAWKMAN USED IN HIS MACE WAS SYNTHETIC...

...SO YOUR SYSTEM SHOULD BE ABLE TO FIGHT IT OFF ON ITS OWN. GIVEN SOME TIME.

SHOULD BE?

WE'RE DEALING WITH A LOT OF UNKNOWNS. BUT BASED ON THE DATA, YOU SHOULD BE FINE.

IT'S LIKE THE EQUIVALEN OF A SUPER FLU AND FOOD POISONING.

FINE. VICTOR, I NEED A WORD WITH YOU. ALONE.

I'LL TAKE THAT AS MY CUE TO LEAVE...

DELETE YOUR ENTIRE DATABASE.

YOU CAN'T REALLY MEAN--

ALL OF IT.

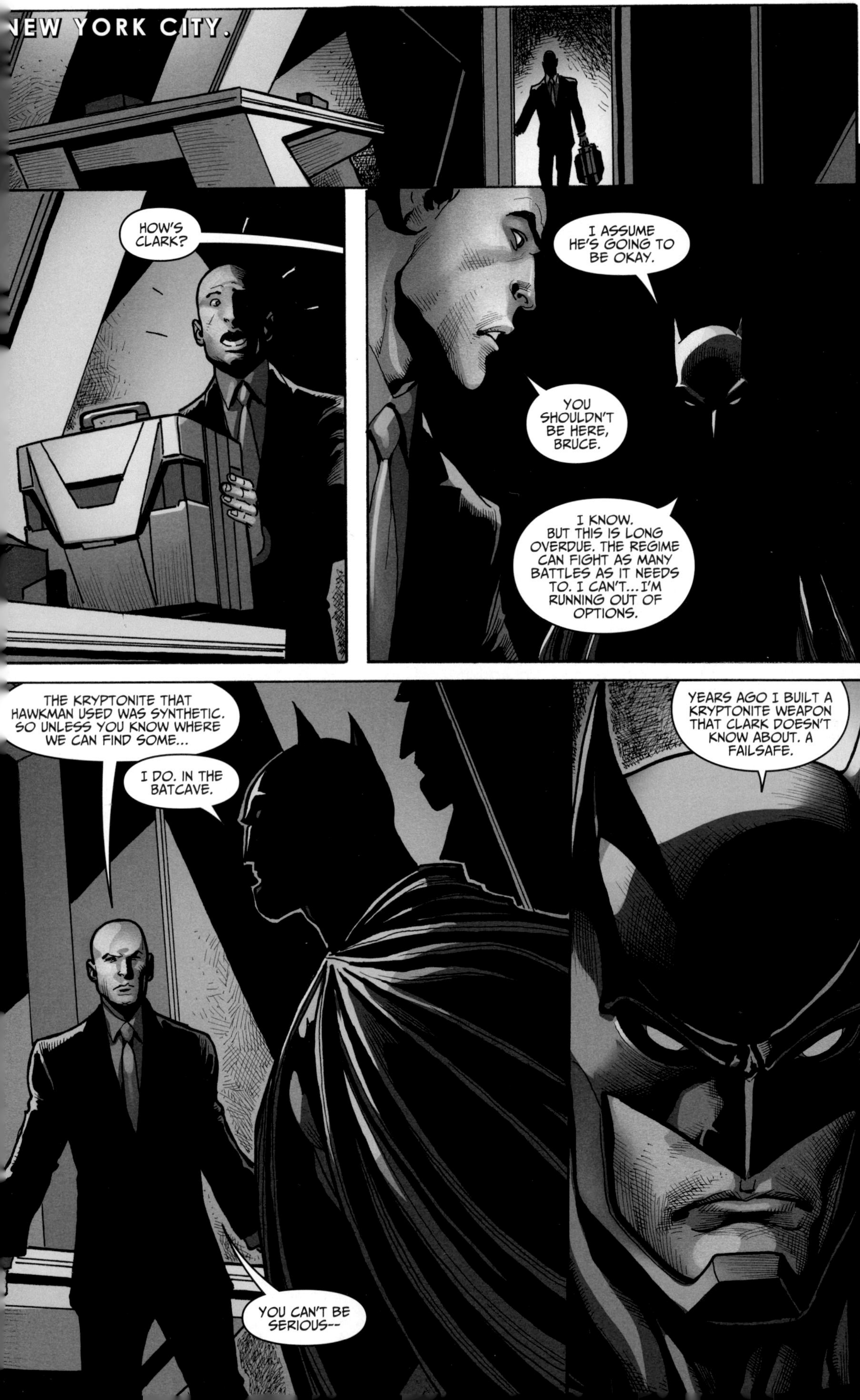
NEW YORK CITY.
HOW'S CLARK?
I ASSUME HE'S GOING TO BE OKAY.
YOU SHOULDN'T BE HERE, BRUCE.
I KNOW. BUT THIS IS LONG OVERDUE. THE REGIME CAN FIGHT AS MANY BATTLES AS IT NEEDS TO. I CAN'T...I'M RUNNING OUT OF OPTIONS.
THE KRYPTONITE THAT HAWKMAN USED WAS SYNTHETIC. SO UNLESS YOU KNOW WHERE WE CAN FIND SOME...
I DO. IN THE BATCAVE.
YOU CAN'T BE SERIOUS--
YEARS AGO I BUILT A KRYPTONITE WEAPON THAT CLARK DOESN'T KNOW ABOUT. A FAILSAFE.

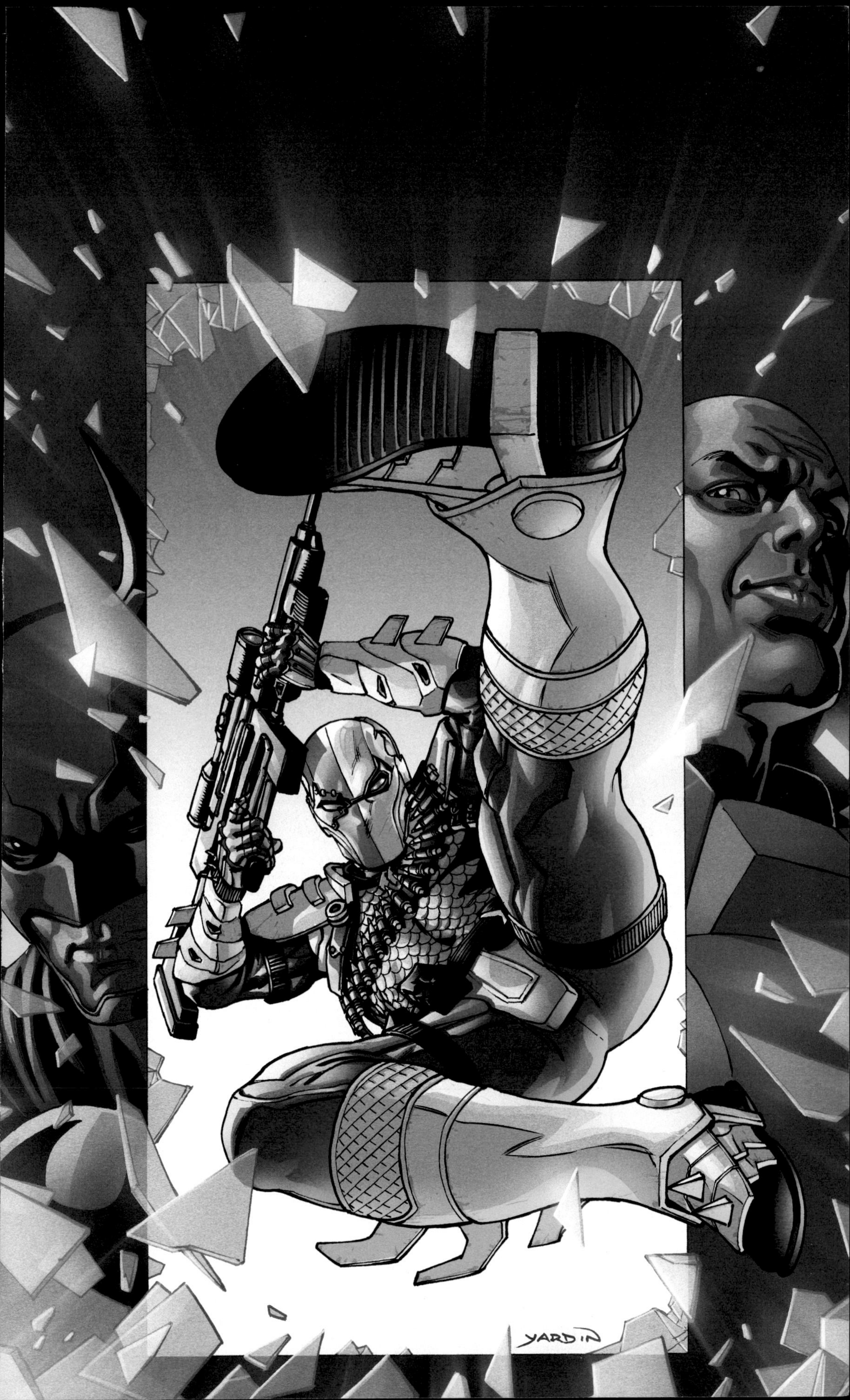
YARDIN

"The Plan" **Mike S. Miller** Artist **J. Nanjan** Colorist

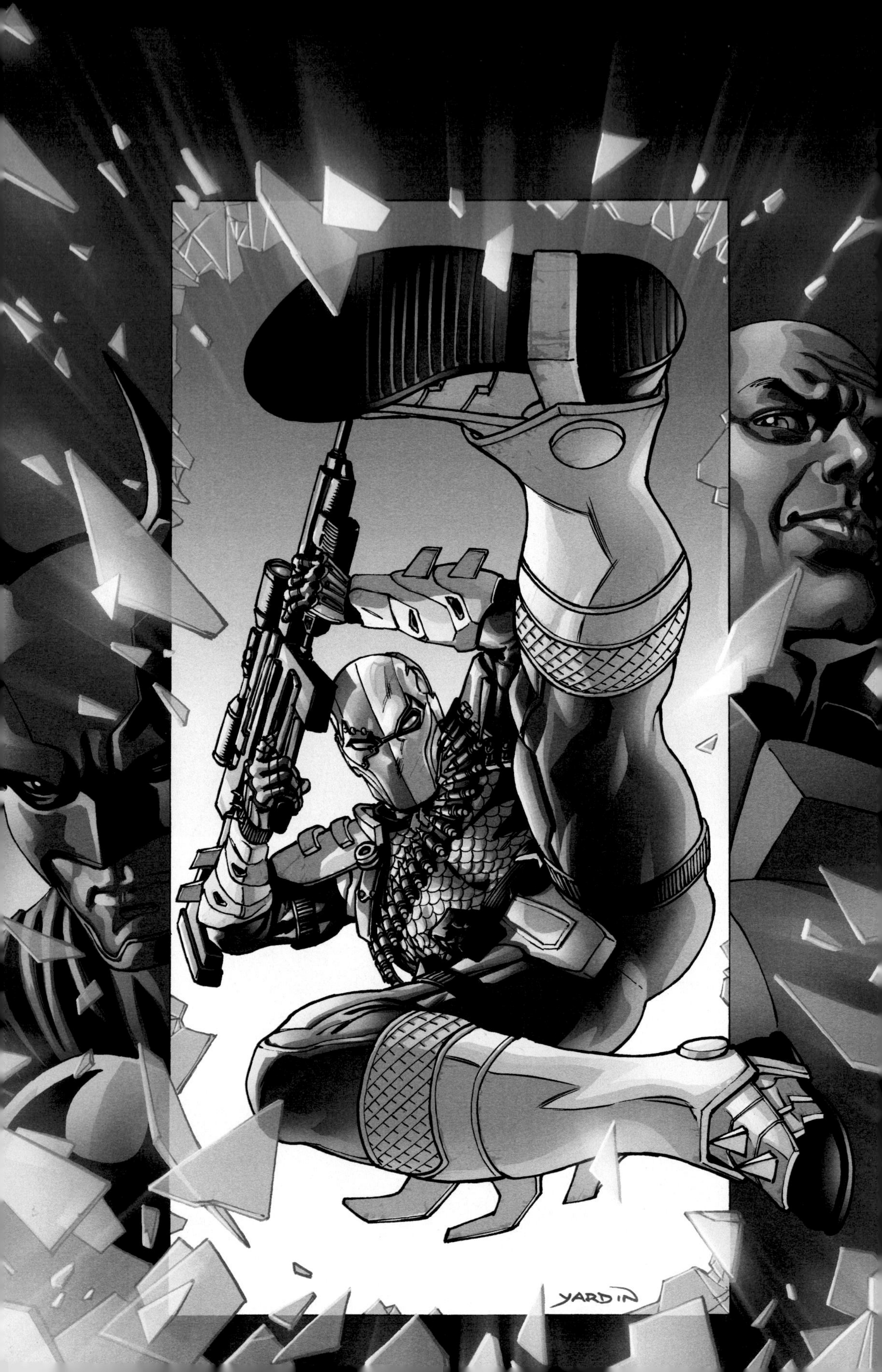
YARDIN

THE PLAN

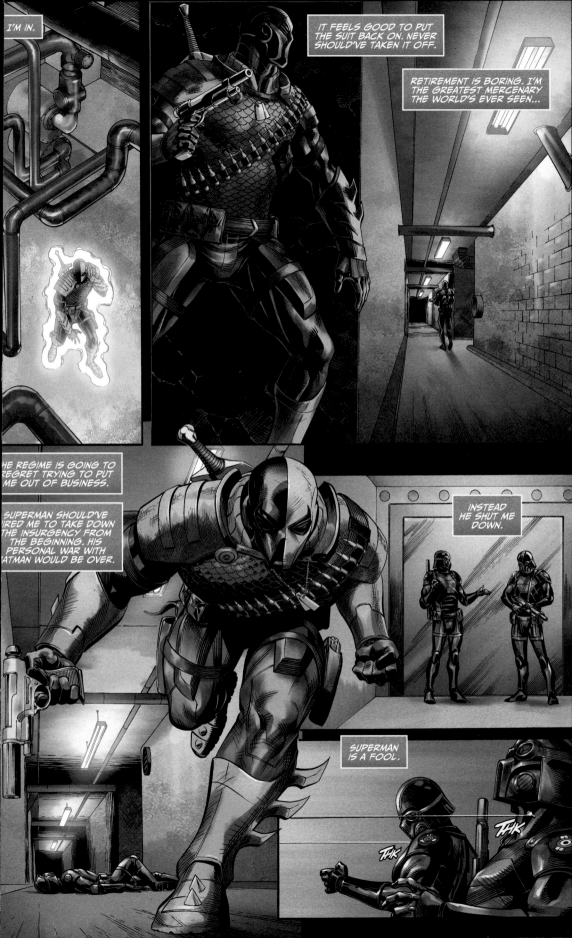

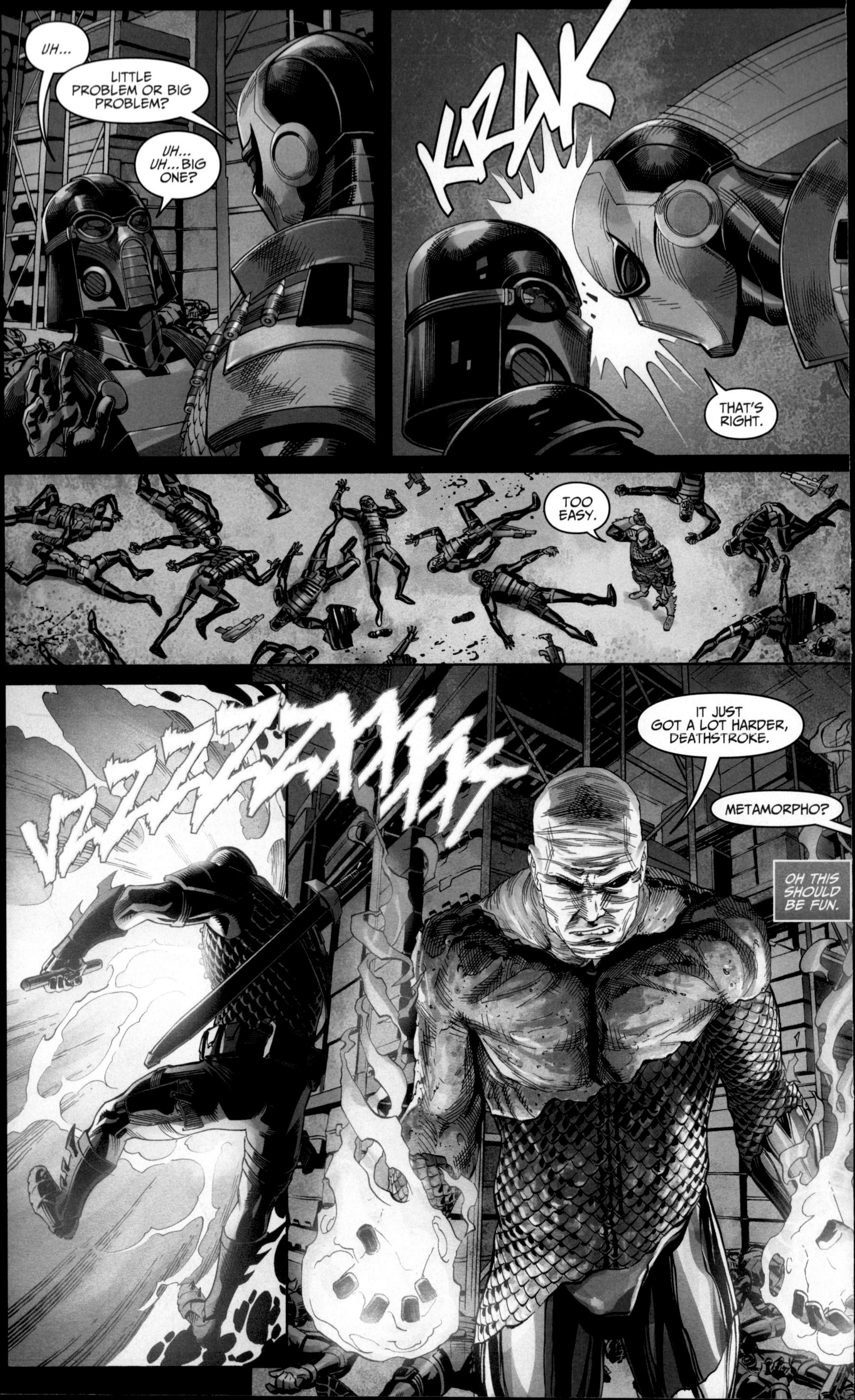
UH...
LITTLE PROBLEM OR BIG PROBLEM?
UH... UH...BIG ONE?
KRAK
THAT'S RIGHT.
TOO EASY.
VZZZZMMS
IT JUST GOT A LOT HARDER, DEATHSTROKE.
METAMORPHO?
OH THIS SHOULD BE FUN.

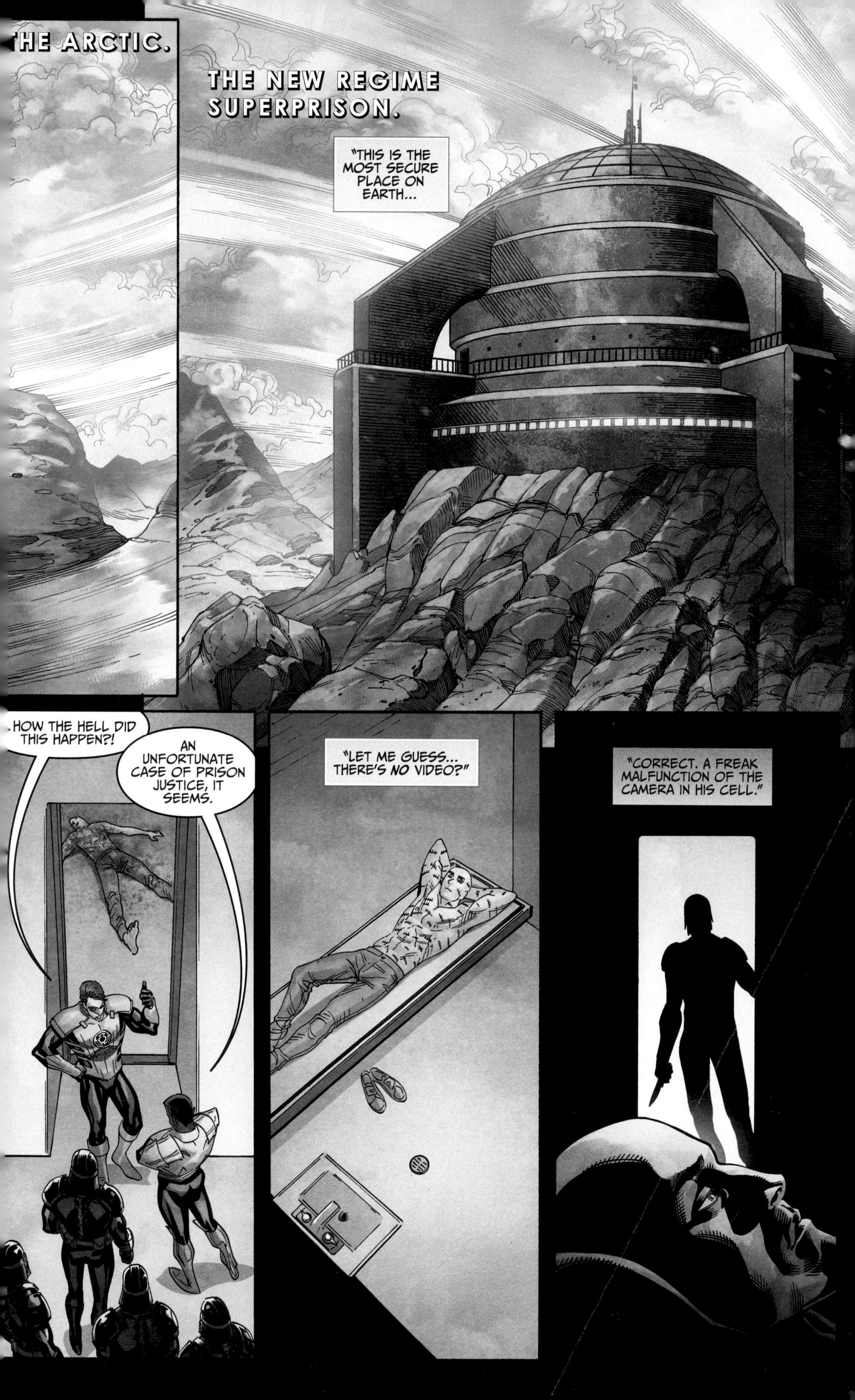
THE ARCTIC.
THE NEW REGIME SUPERPRISON.
"THIS IS THE MOST SECURE PLACE ON EARTH...
...HOW THE HELL DID THIS HAPPEN?!
AN UNFORTUNATE CASE OF PRISON JUSTICE, IT SEEMS.
"LET ME GUESS... THERE'S NO VIDEO?"
"CORRECT. A FREAK MALFUNCTION OF THE CAMERA IN HIS CELL."

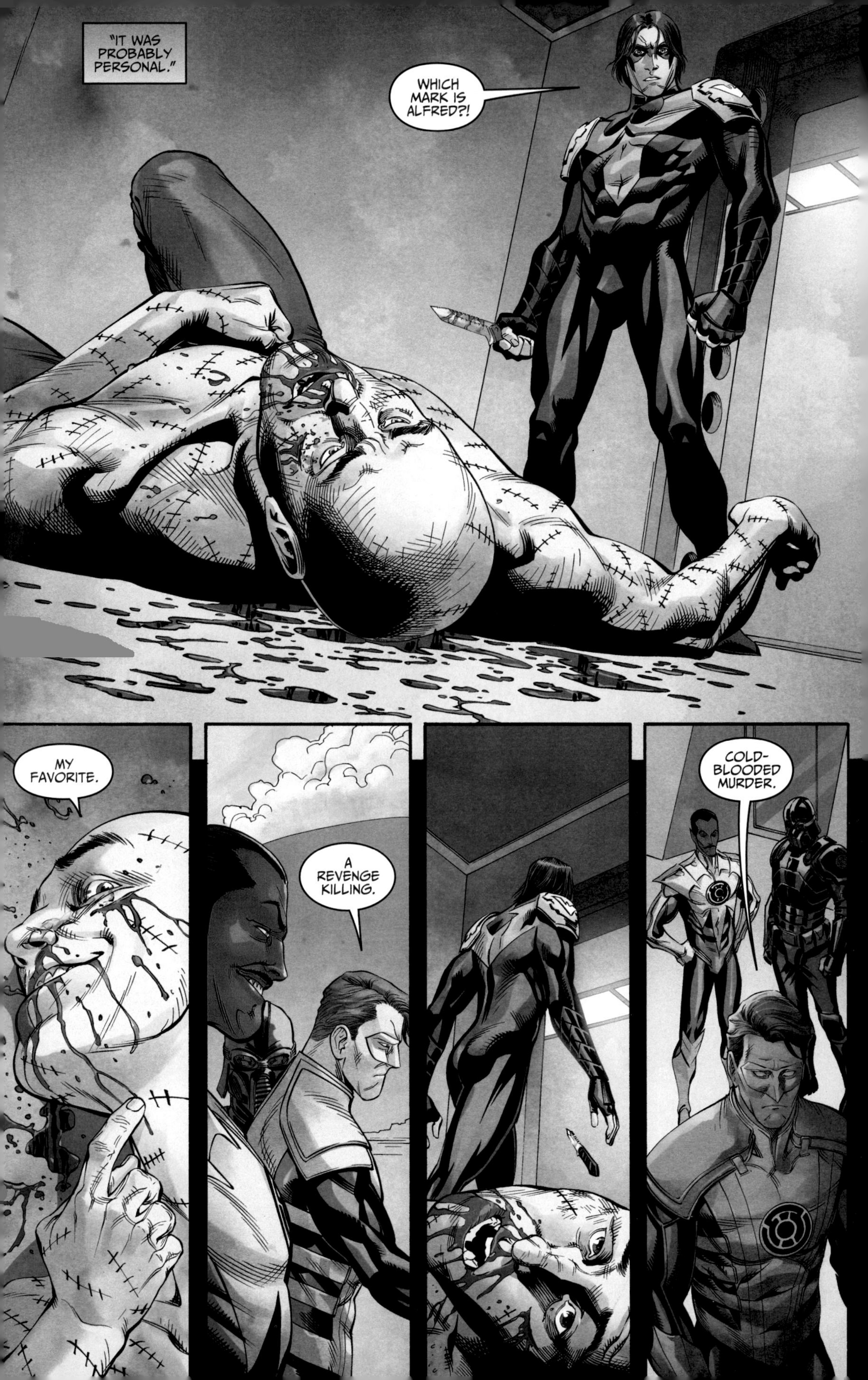
"IT WAS PROBABLY PERSONAL."
WHICH MARK IS ALFRED?!
MY FAVORITE.
A REVENGE KILLING.
COLD-BLOODED MURDER.

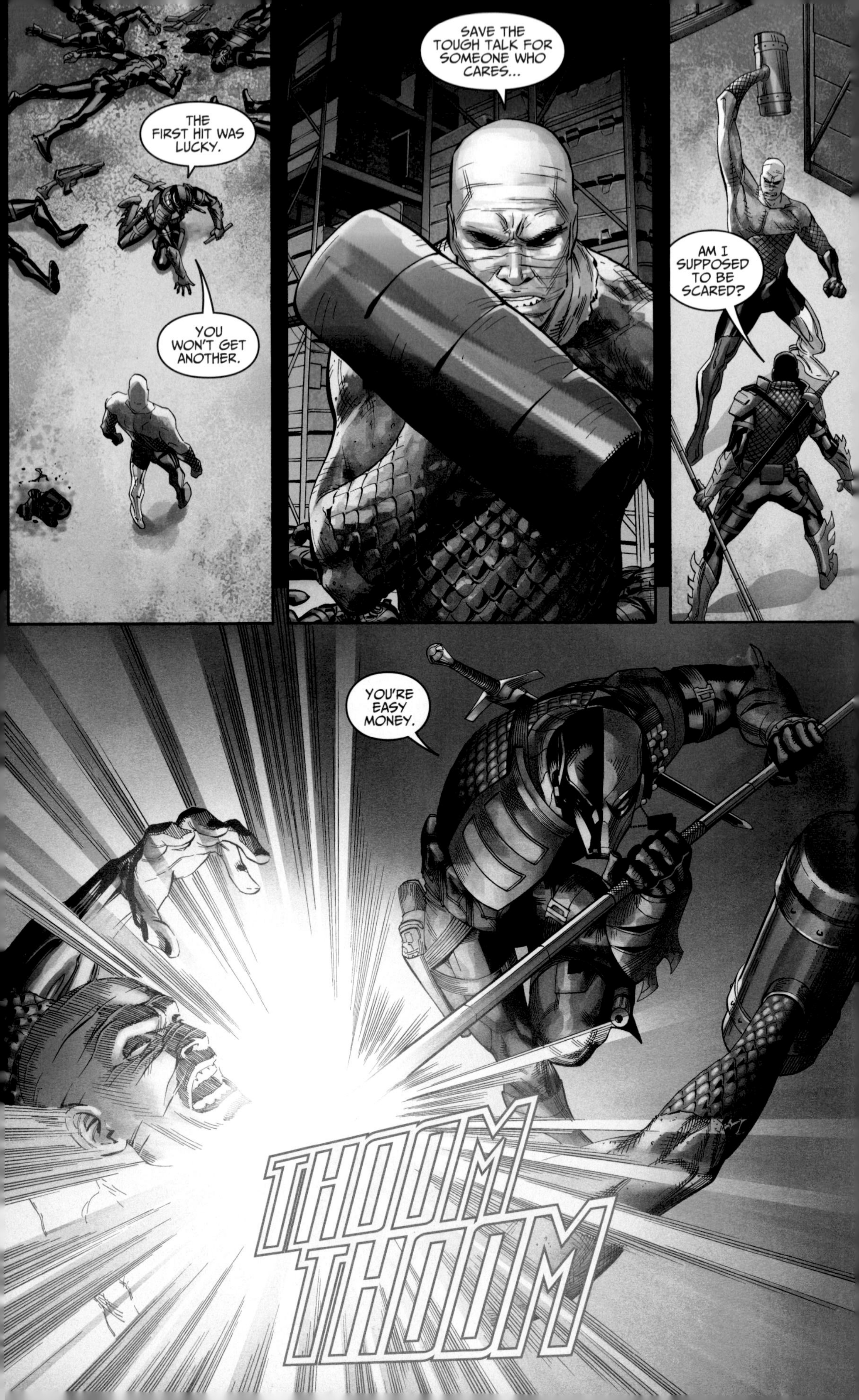
THE FIRST HIT WAS LUCKY.
YOU WON'T GET ANOTHER.
SAVE THE TOUGH TALK FOR SOMEONE WHO CARES...
AM I SUPPOSED TO BE SCARED?
YOU'RE EASY MONEY.
THOOM THOOM

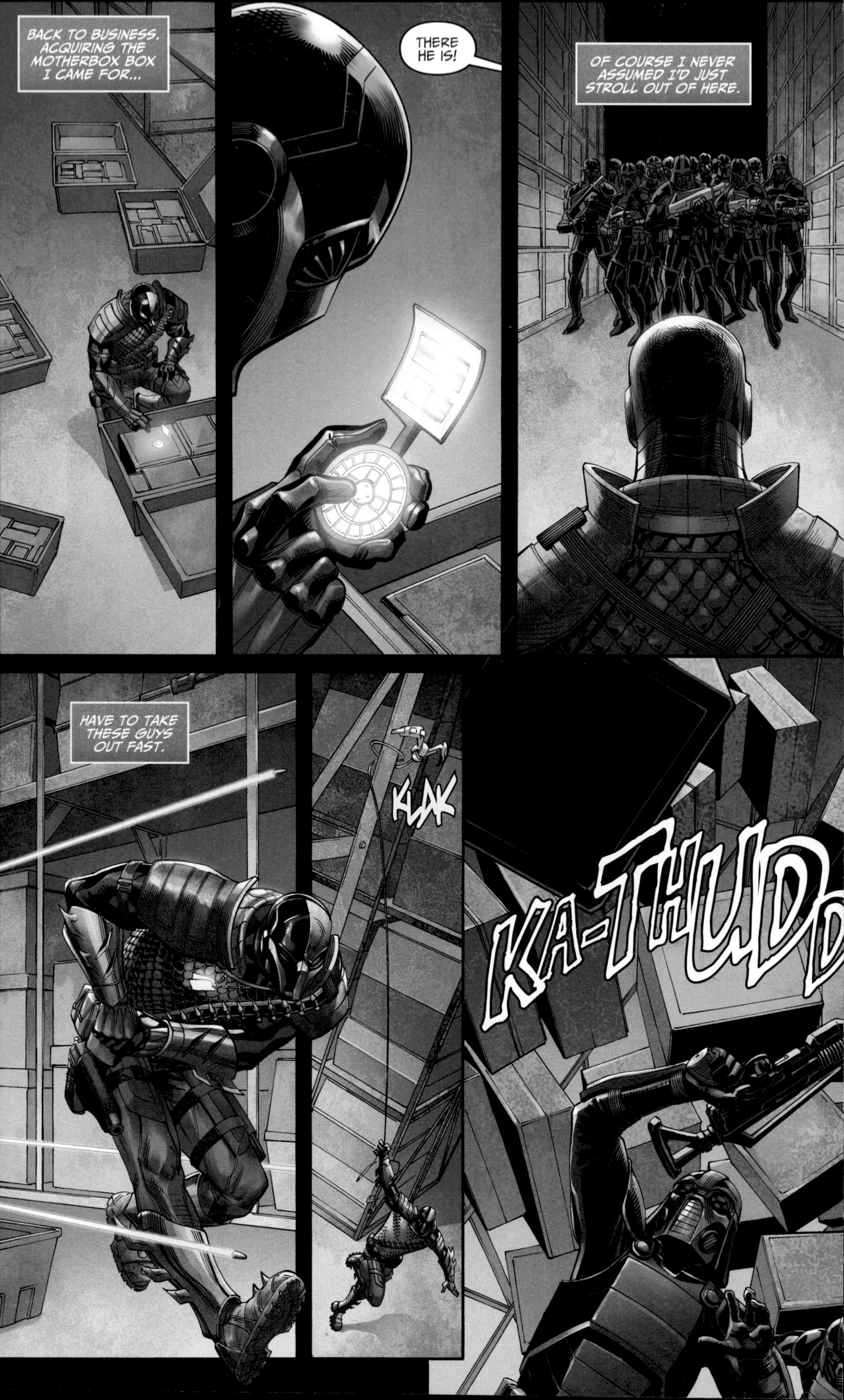
BACK TO BUSINESS. ACQUIRING THE MOTHERBOX BOX I CAME FOR...
THERE HE IS!
OF COURSE I NEVER ASSUMED I'D JUST STROLL OUT OF HERE.
HAVE TO TAKE THESE GUYS OUT FAST.
KLAK
KA-THUDD

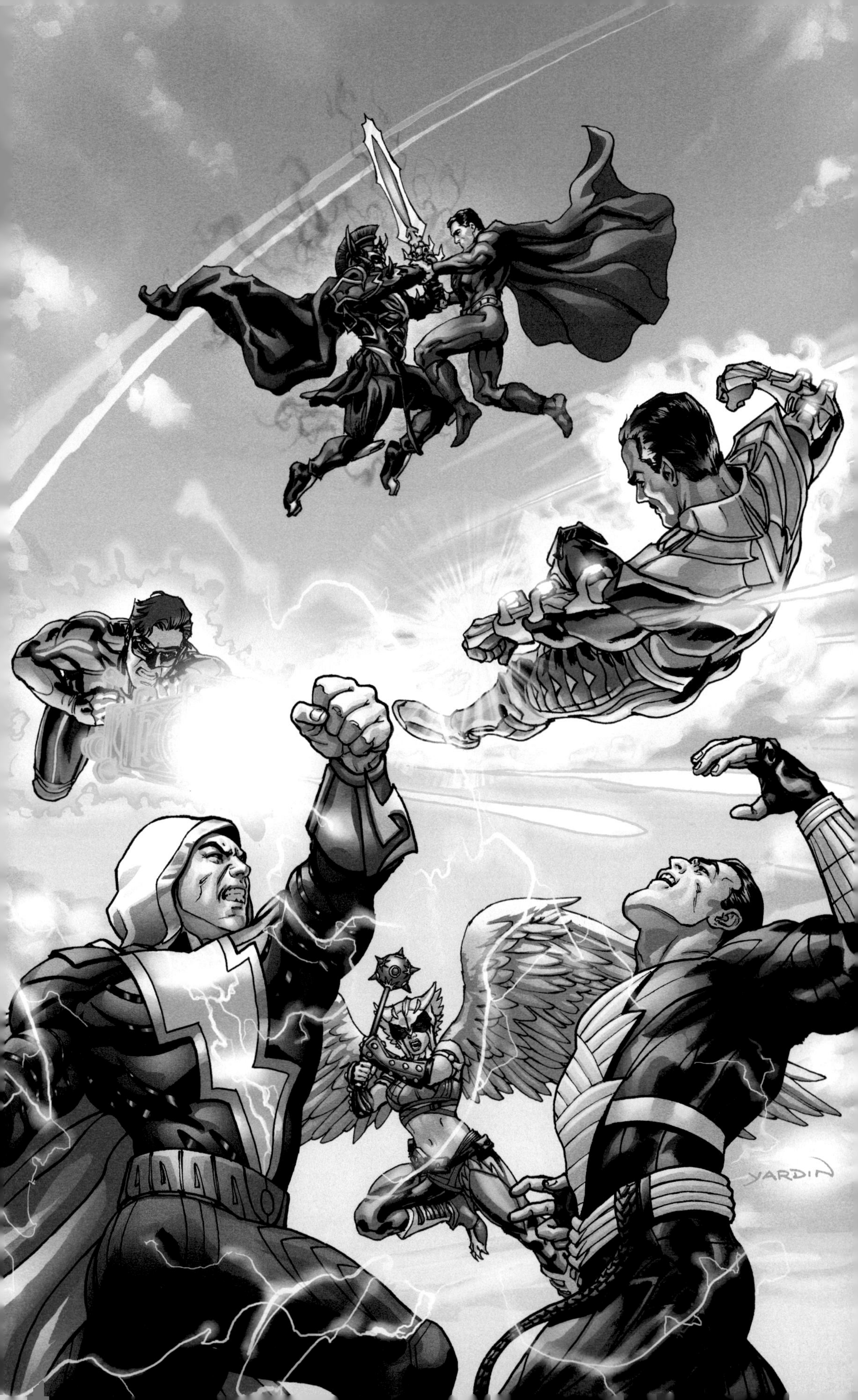
YARDIN

"A Better World" **Xermanico** Artist **Rex Lokus** Colorist
"Funsies" **Marco Santucci** Artist **Rex Lokus** Colorist

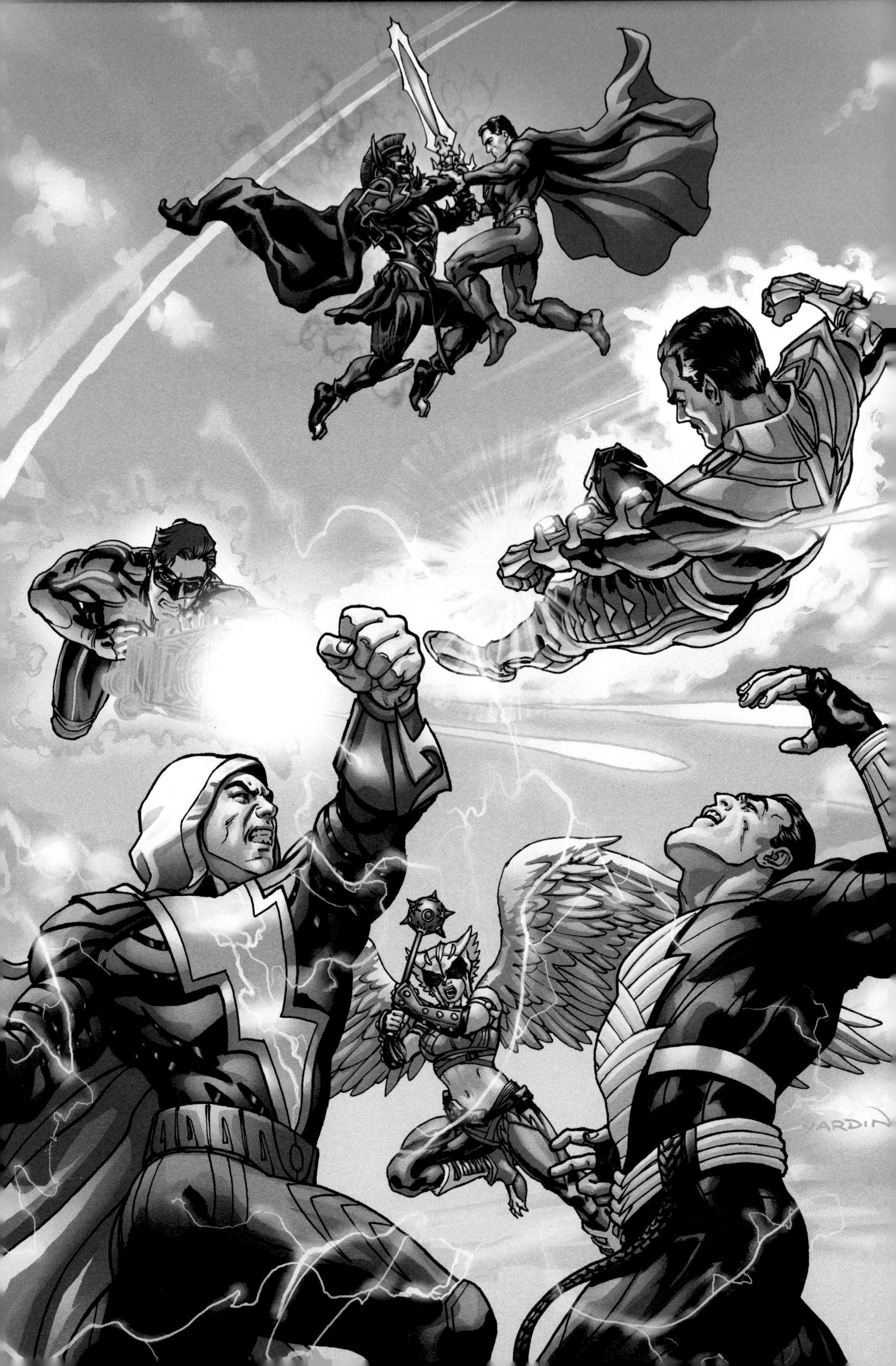
YARDIN

THE MOST AMAZING SOUND I'VE EVER HEARD, MA...

...TWO HEARTBEATS.

WE'RE GOING TO HAVE A BABY.

THAT'S FANTASTIC. HOW DO YOU FEEL, LOIS?

I'M FINE. *HE'S* PETRIFIED.

I'M NOT PETRIFIED.

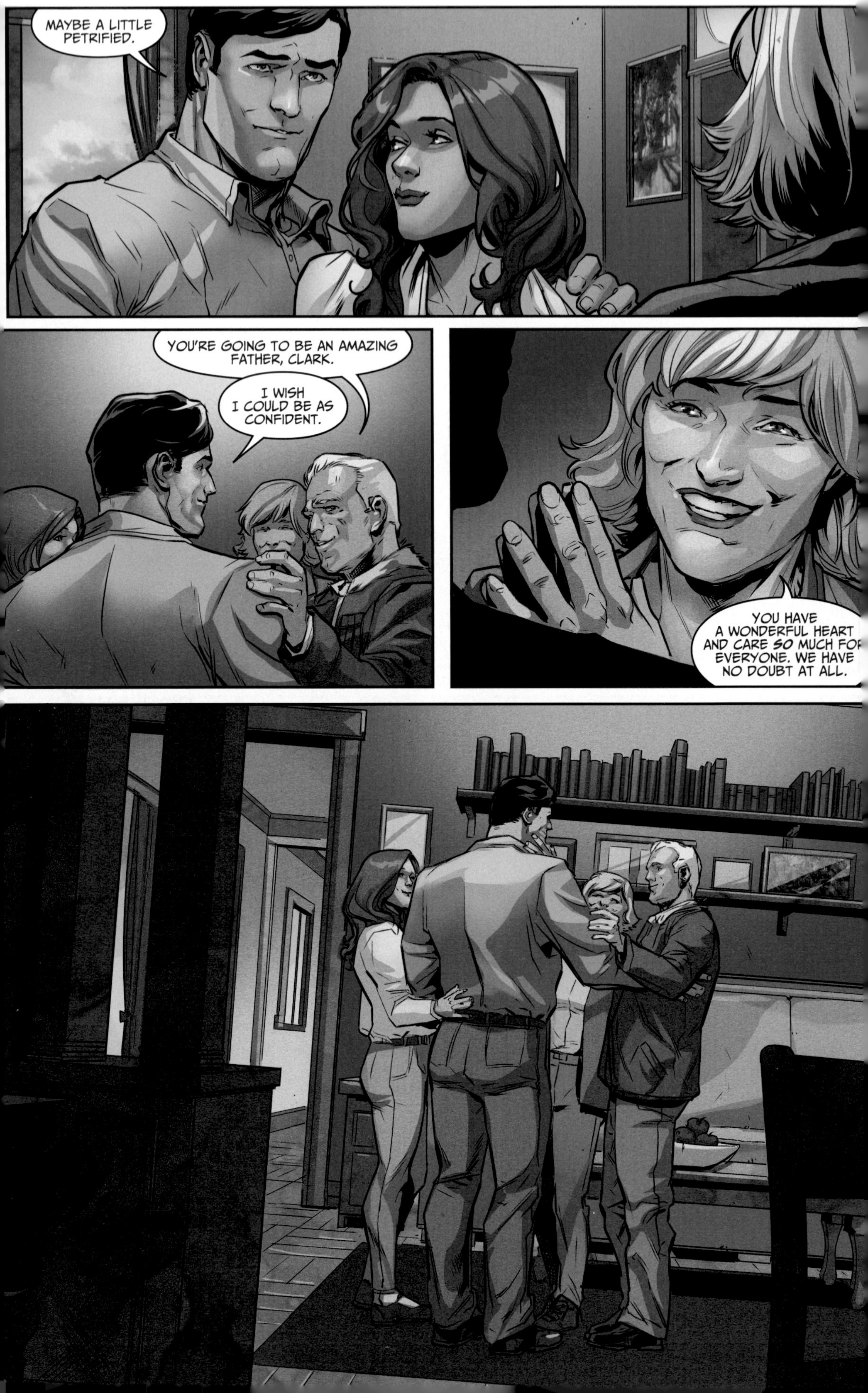
MAYBE A LITTLE PETRIFIED.
YOU'RE GOING TO BE AN AMAZING FATHER, CLARK.
I WISH I COULD BE AS CONFIDENT.
YOU HAVE A WONDERFUL HEART AND CARE SO MUCH FOR EVERYONE. WE HAVE NO DOUBT AT ALL.

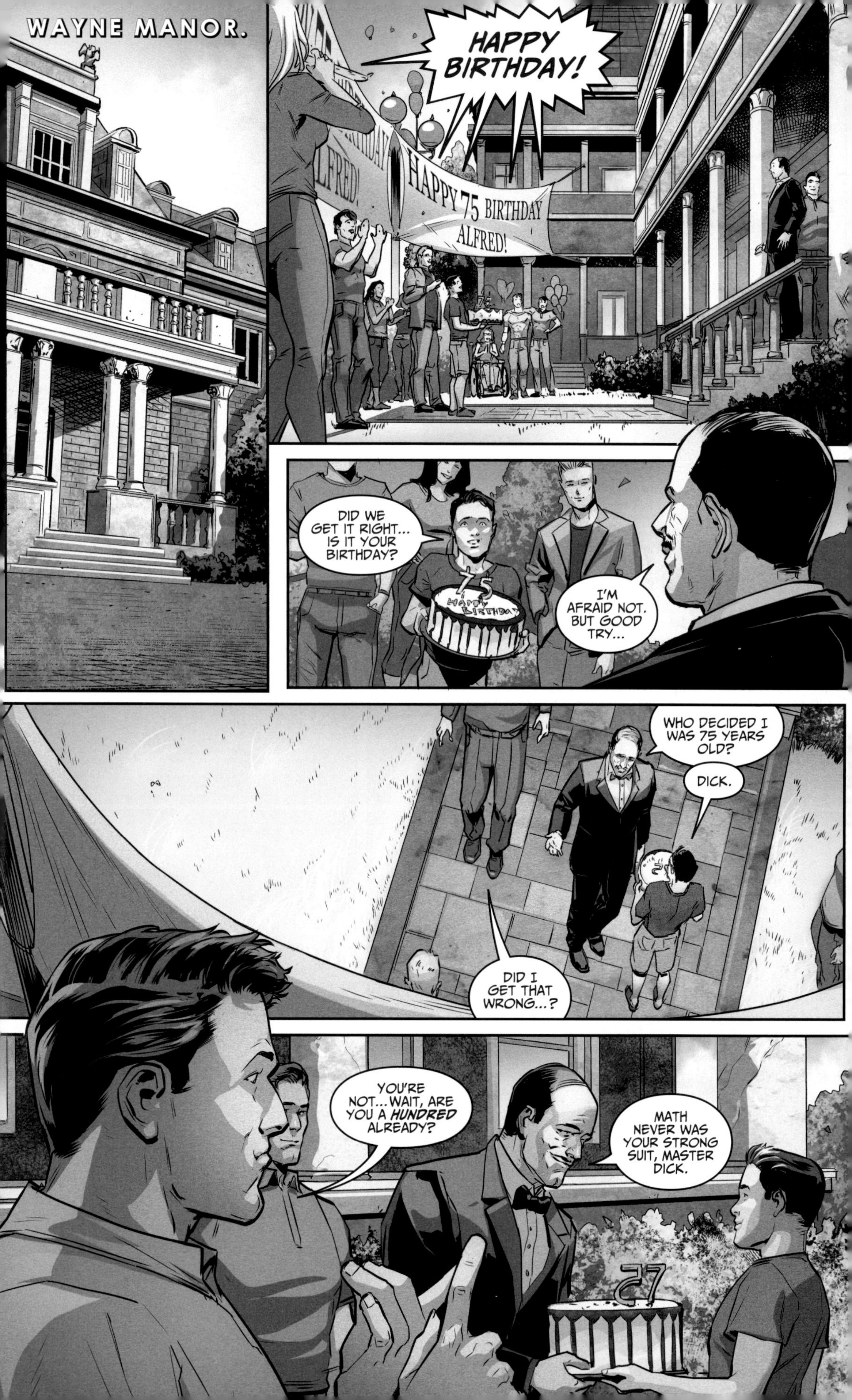
WAYNE MANOR.
HAPPY BIRTHDAY!
HAPPY 75 BIRTHDAY ALFRED!
DID WE GET IT RIGHT... IS IT YOUR BIRTHDAY?
HAPPY BIRTHDAY
I'M AFRAID NOT. BUT GOOD TRY...
WHO DECIDED I WAS 75 YEARS OLD?
DICK.
DID I GET THAT WRONG...?
YOU'RE NOT...WAIT, ARE YOU A *HUNDRED* ALREADY?
MATH NEVER WAS YOUR STRONG SUIT, MASTER DICK.

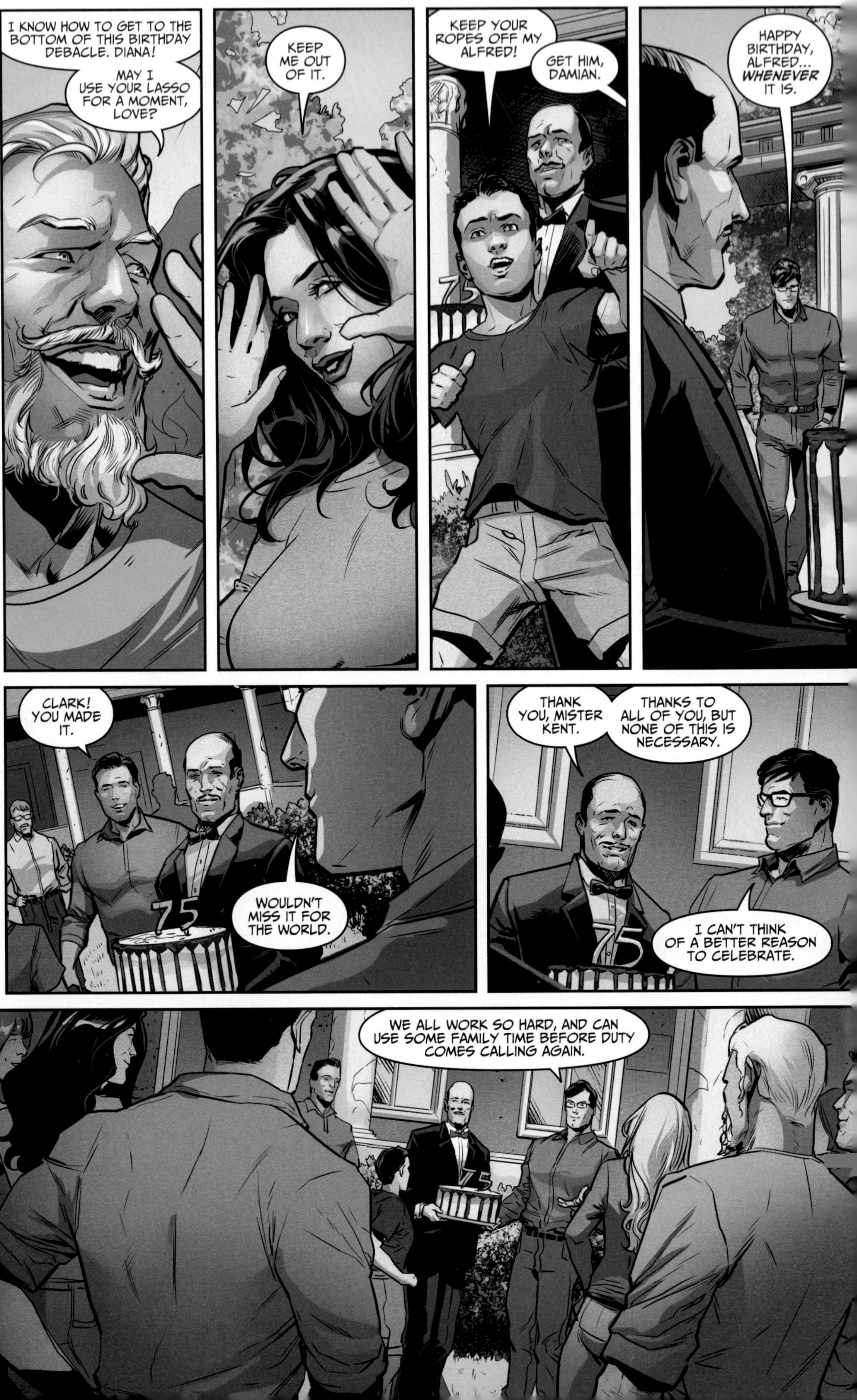
I KNOW HOW TO GET TO THE BOTTOM OF THIS BIRTHDAY DEBACLE. DIANA!
MAY I USE YOUR LASSO FOR A MOMENT, LOVE?
KEEP ME OUT OF IT.
KEEP YOUR ROPES OFF MY ALFRED!
GET HIM, DAMIAN.
HAPPY BIRTHDAY, ALFRED... *WHENEVER* IT IS.
CLARK! YOU MADE IT.
WOULDN'T MISS IT FOR THE WORLD.
THANK YOU, MISTER KENT.
THANKS TO ALL OF YOU, BUT NONE OF THIS IS NECESSARY.
I CAN'T THINK OF A BETTER REASON TO CELEBRATE.
WE ALL WORK SO HARD, AND CAN USE SOME FAMILY TIME BEFORE DUTY COMES CALLING AGAIN.

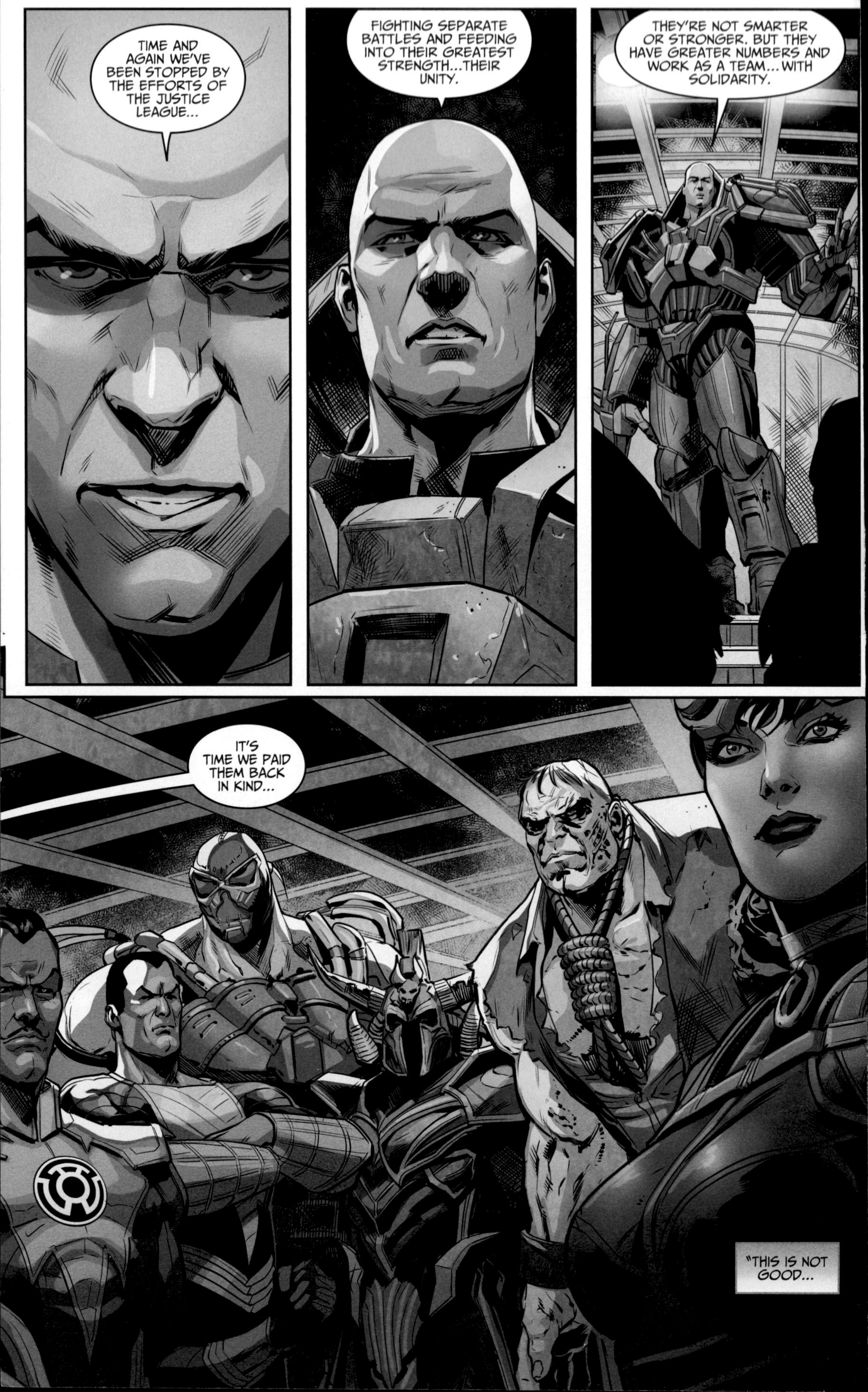
TIME AND AGAIN WE'VE BEEN STOPPED BY THE EFFORTS OF THE JUSTICE LEAGUE...
FIGHTING SEPARATE BATTLES AND FEEDING INTO THEIR GREATEST STRENGTH...THEIR UNITY.
THEY'RE NOT SMARTER OR STRONGER. BUT THEY HAVE GREATER NUMBERS AND WORK AS A TEAM...WITH SOLIDARITY.
IT'S TIME WE PAID THEM BACK IN KIND...
"THIS IS NOT GOOD...

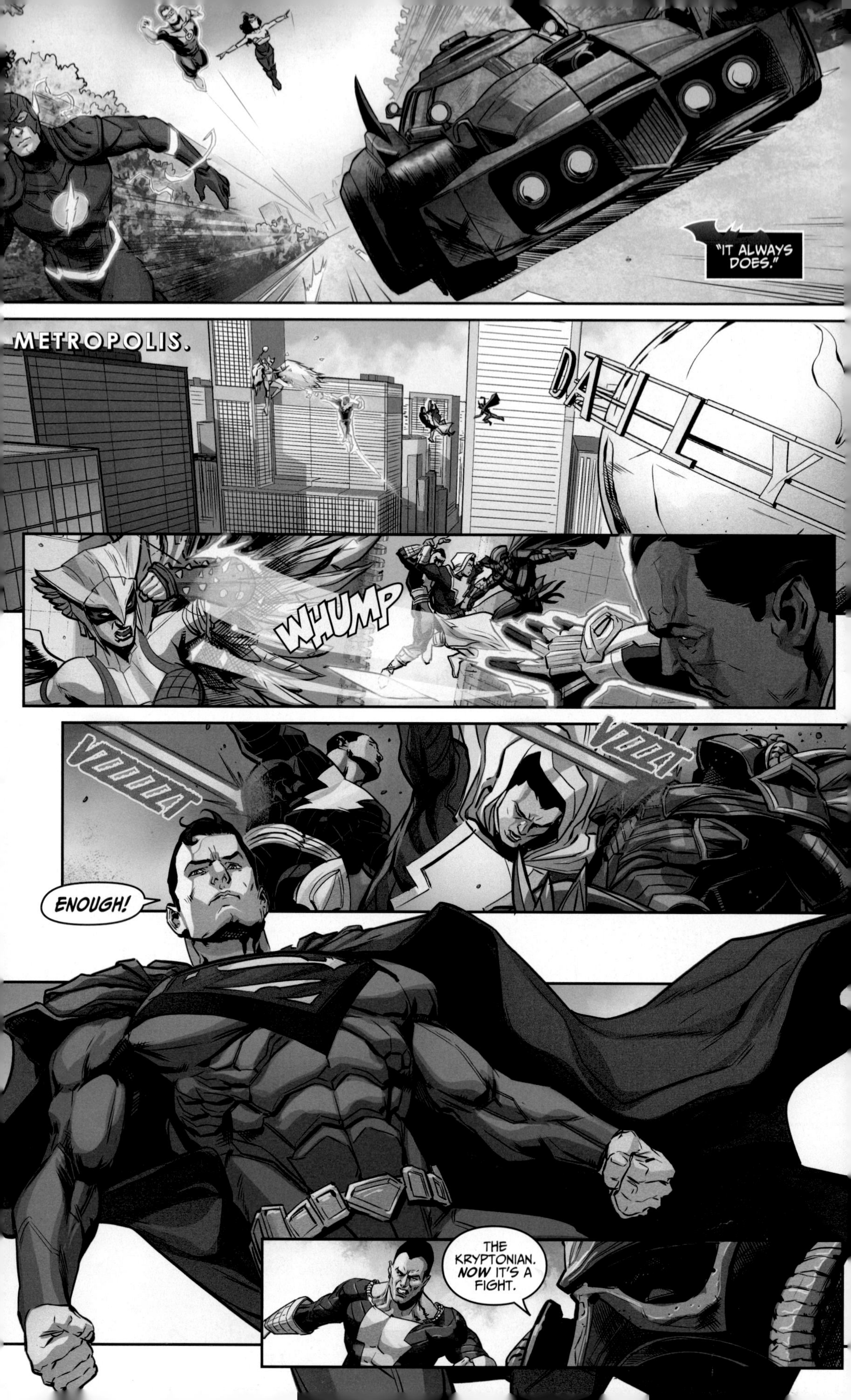
"IT ALWAYS DOES."
METROPOLIS.
DAILY
WHUMP
VZZZT
VZZZT
ENOUGH!
THE KRYPTONIAN. NOW IT'S A FIGHT.

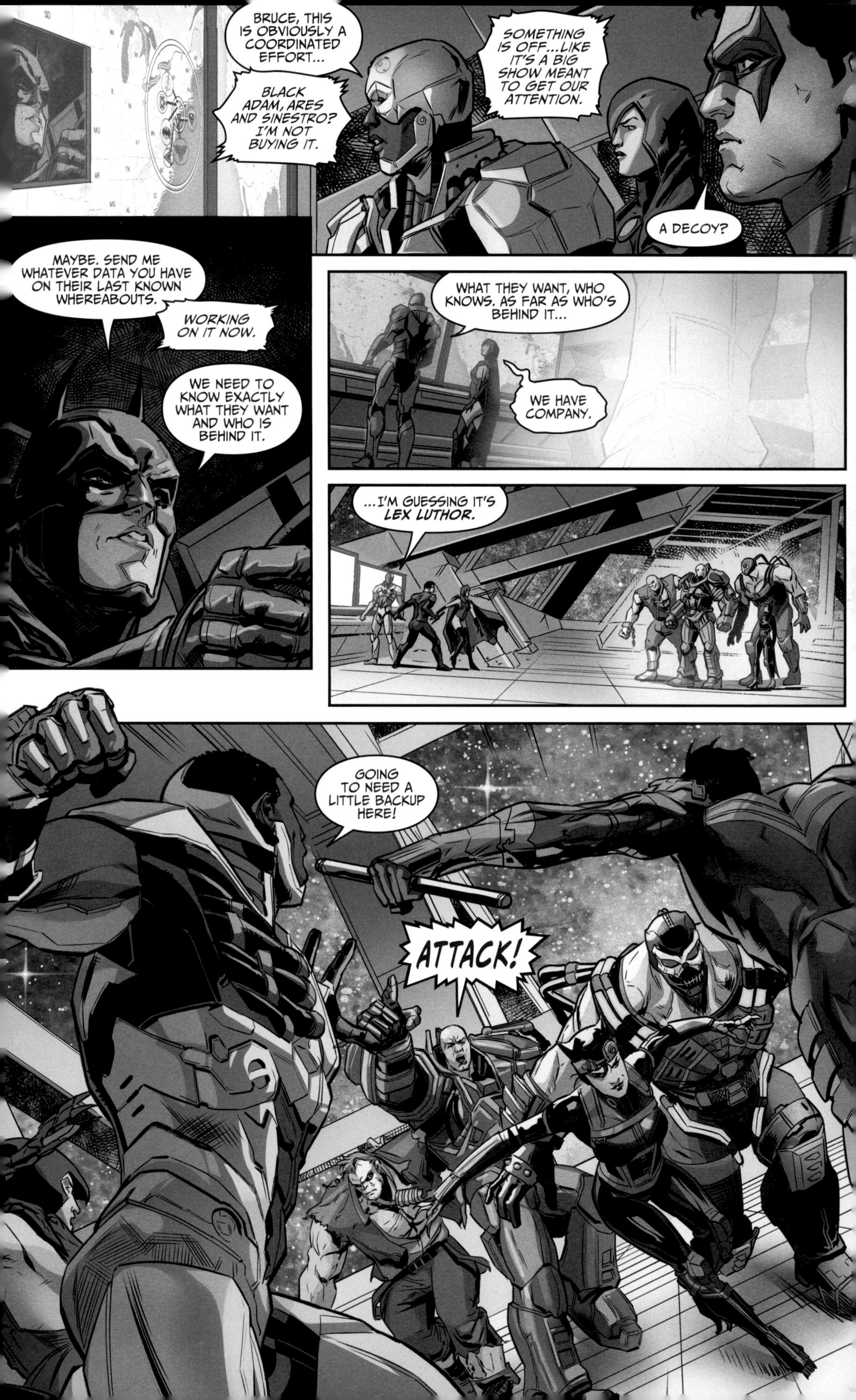
BRUCE, THIS IS OBVIOUSLY A COORDINATED EFFORT...
BLACK ADAM, ARES AND SINESTRO? I'M NOT BUYING IT.
SOMETHING IS OFF...LIKE IT'S A BIG SHOW MEANT TO GET OUR ATTENTION.
A DECOY?
MAYBE. SEND ME WHATEVER DATA YOU HAVE ON THEIR LAST KNOWN WHEREABOUTS.
WORKING ON IT NOW.
WE NEED TO KNOW EXACTLY WHAT THEY WANT AND WHO IS BEHIND IT.
WHAT THEY WANT, WHO KNOWS. AS FAR AS WHO'S BEHIND IT...
WE HAVE COMPANY.
...I'M GUESSING IT'S LEX LUTHOR.
GOING TO NEED A LITTLE BACKUP HERE!
ATTACK!

WE'RE KEEPIN' A CLOSE EYE ON *JOKER*, JUST LIKE YOU SAID.

HE HASN'T MOVED IN HOURS.

CELL-A4

CAREFUL.

LOOK.

A TRIPWIRE.

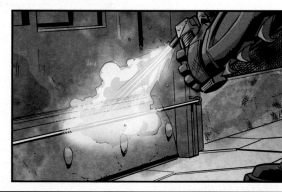

JOKER'S... GONE?!

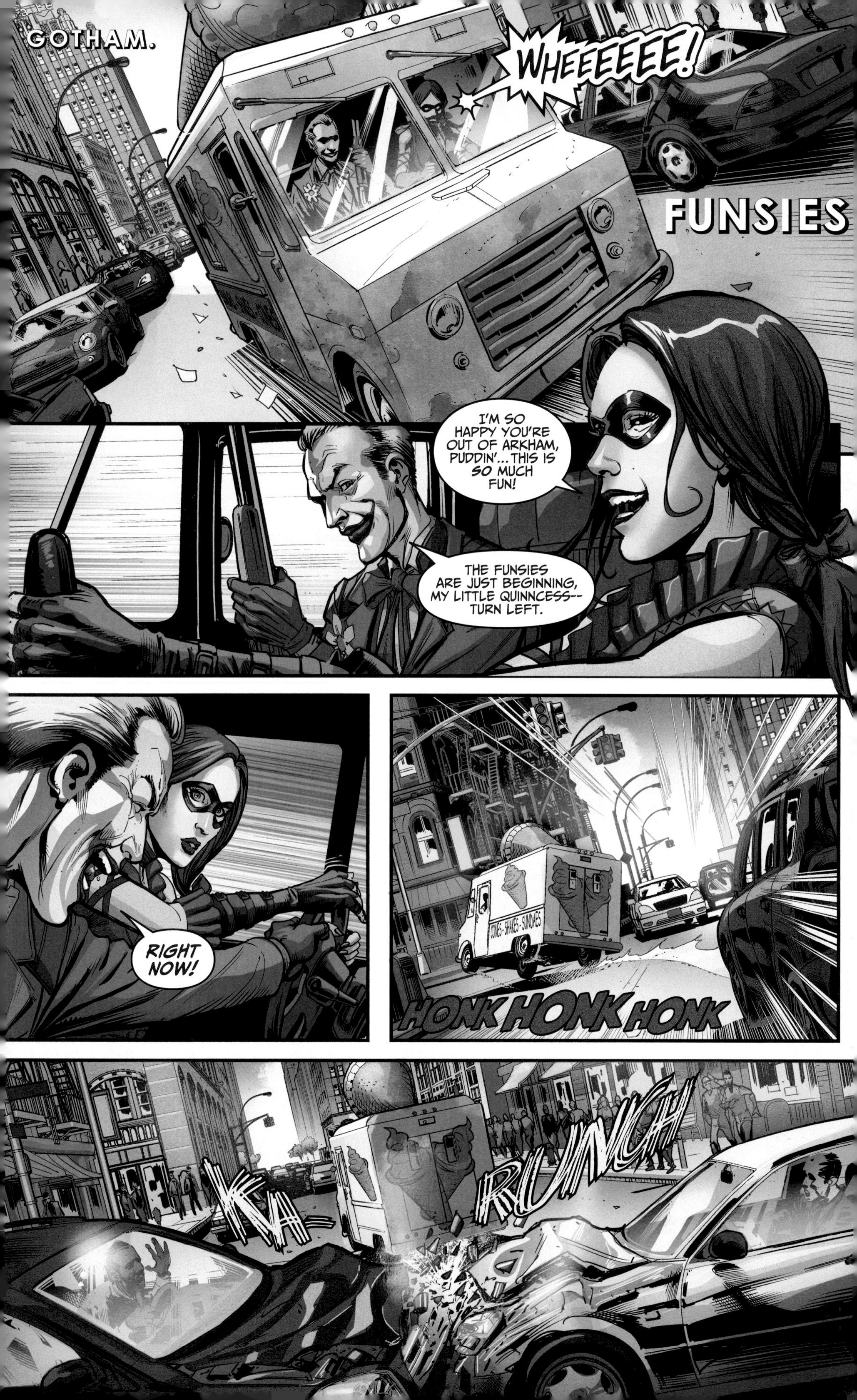
GOTHAM.
WHEEEEEE!
FUNSIES
I'M SO HAPPY YOU'RE OUT OF ARKHAM, PUDDIN'...THIS IS SO MUCH FUN!
THE FUNSIES ARE JUST BEGINNING, MY LITTLE QUINNCESS--TURN LEFT.
RIGHT NOW!
CONES - SHAKES - SUNDAES
HONK HONK HONK
KA-RUNCH

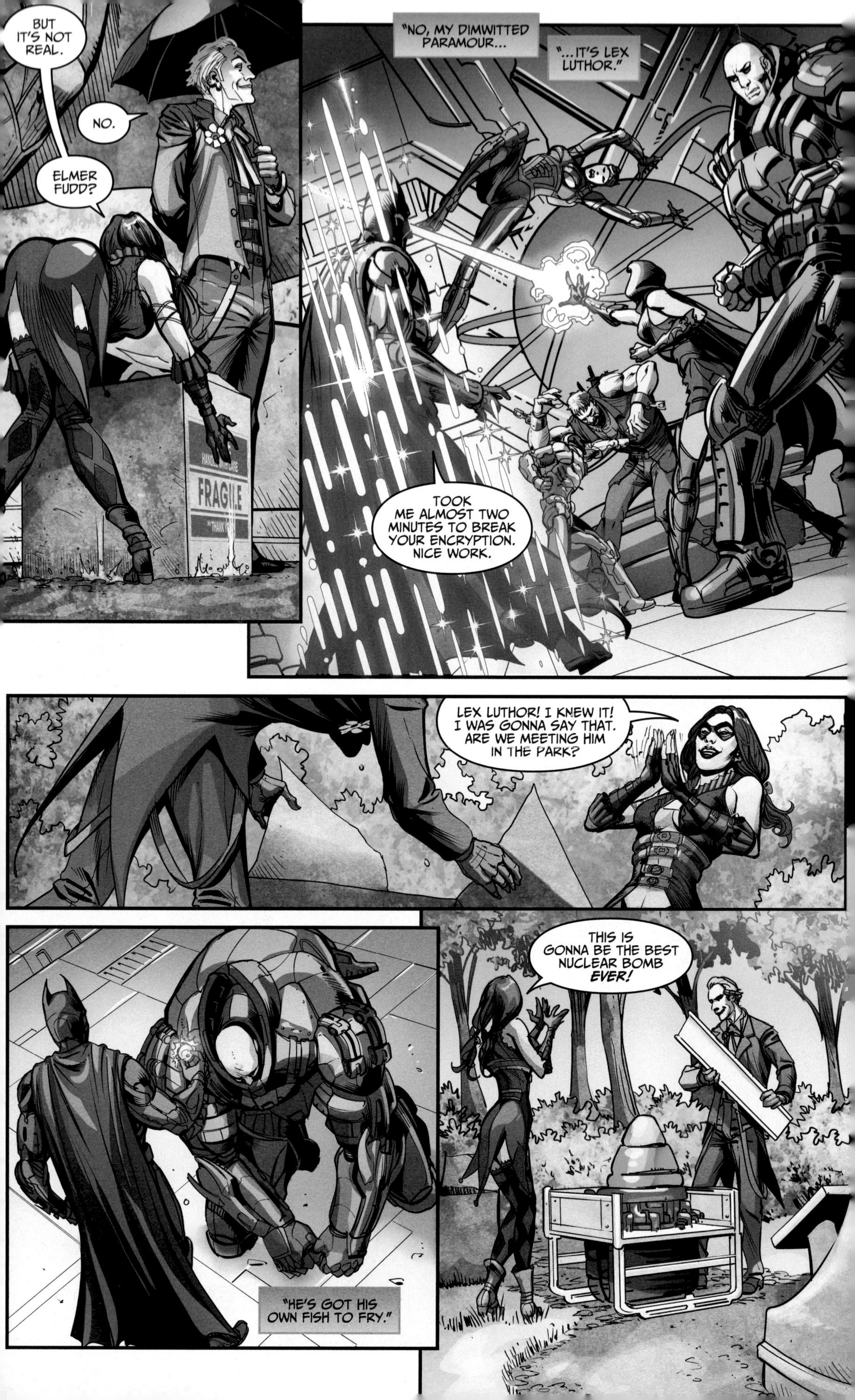
BUT IT'S NOT REAL.
NO.
ELMER FUDD?
"NO, MY DIMWITTED PARAMOUR...
"...IT'S LEX LUTHOR."
TOOK ME ALMOST TWO MINUTES TO BREAK YOUR ENCRYPTION. NICE WORK.
HANDLE WITH CARE
FRAGILE
LEX LUTHOR! I KNEW IT! I WAS GONNA SAY THAT. ARE WE MEETING HIM IN THE PARK?
"HE'S GOT HIS OWN FISH TO FRY."
THIS IS GONNA BE THE BEST NUCLEAR BOMB *EVER!*

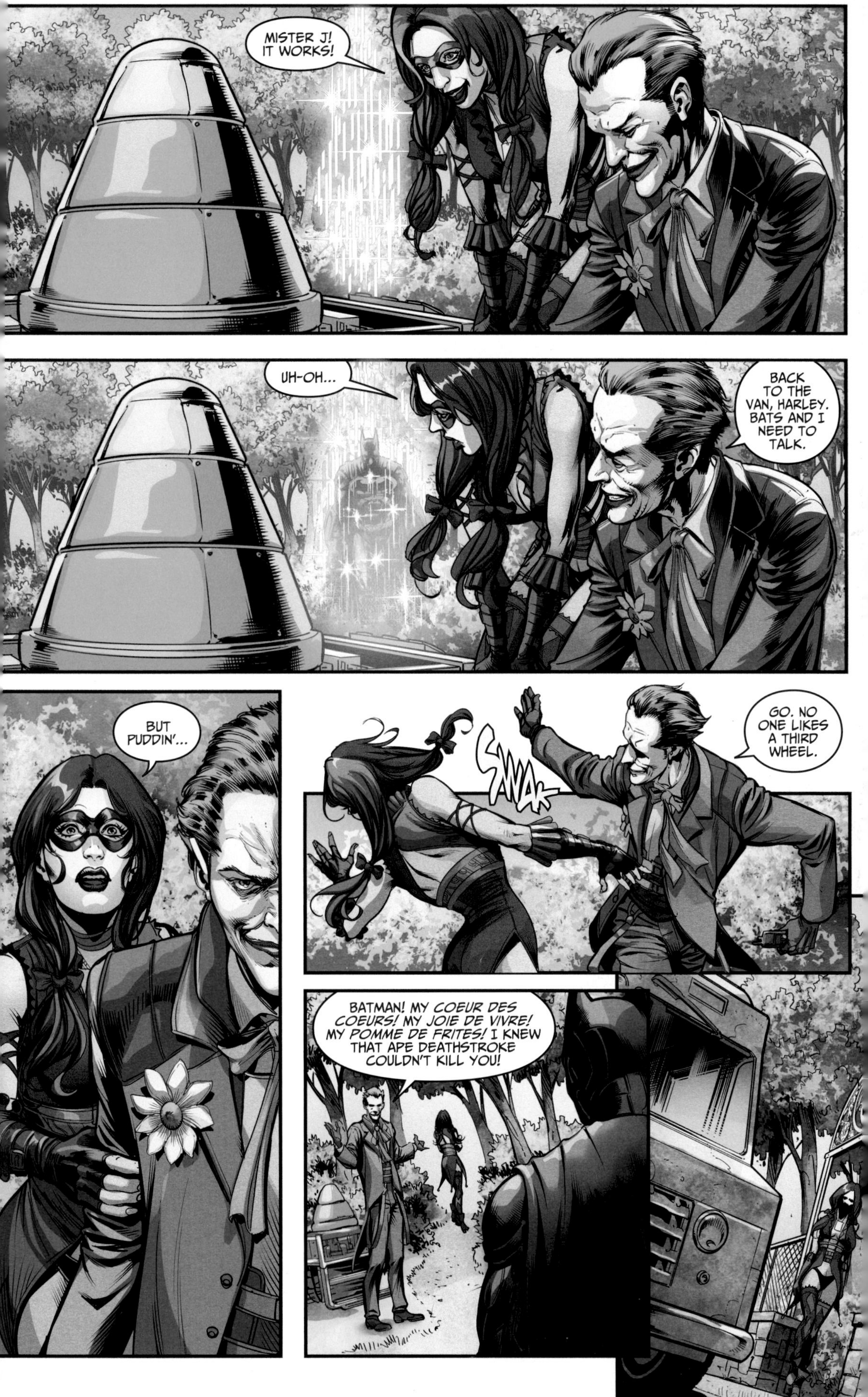
MISTER J! IT WORKS!
UH-OH...
BACK TO THE VAN, HARLEY. BATS AND I NEED TO TALK.
BUT PUDDIN'...
SMAK
GO. NO ONE LIKES A THIRD WHEEL.
BATMAN! MY COEUR DES COEURS! MY JOIE DE VIVRE! MY POMME DE FRITES! I KNEW THAT APE DEATHSTROKE COULDN'T KILL YOU!

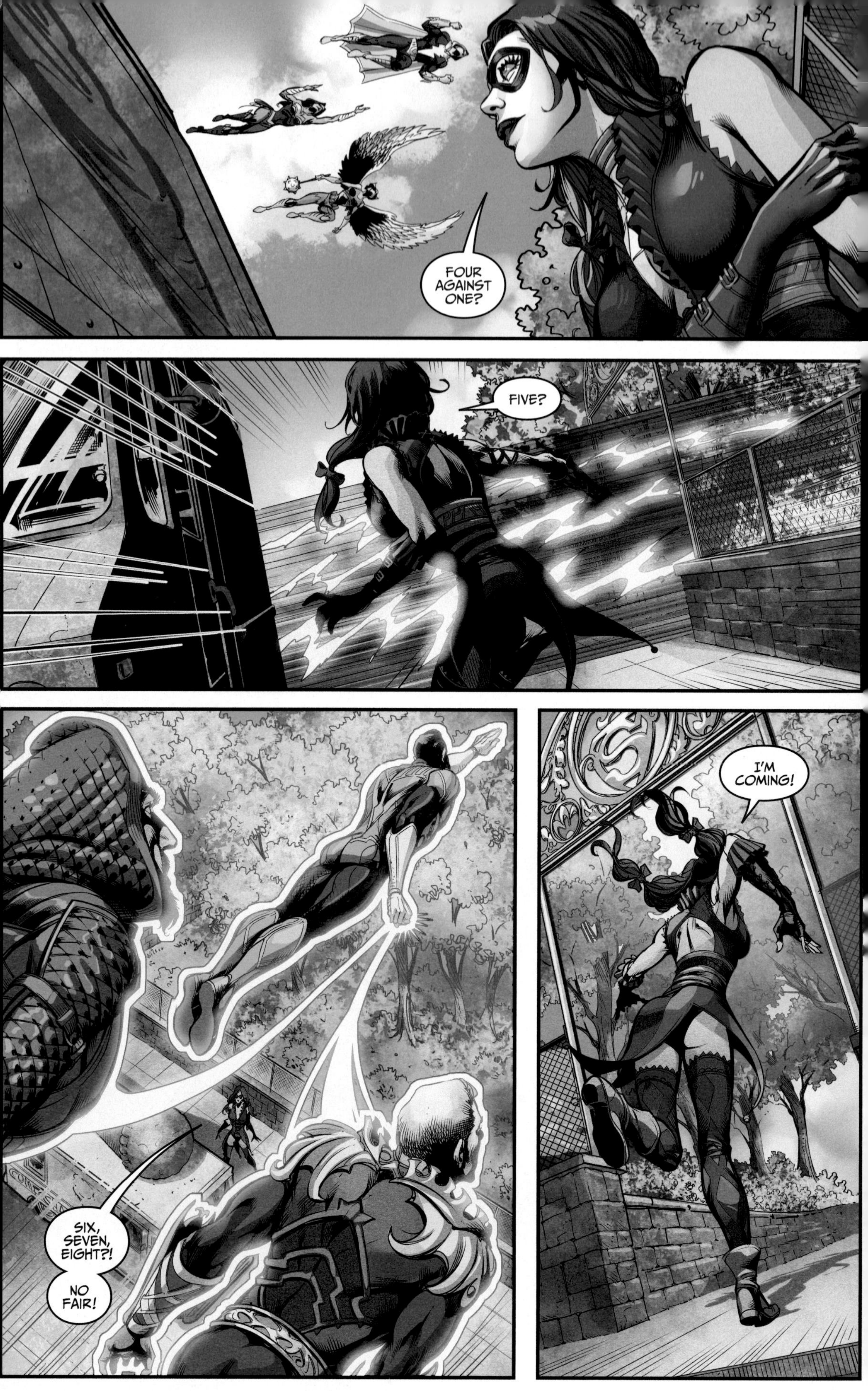
FOUR AGAINST ONE?
FIVE?
SIX, SEVEN, EIGHT?!
NO FAIR!
I'M COMING!

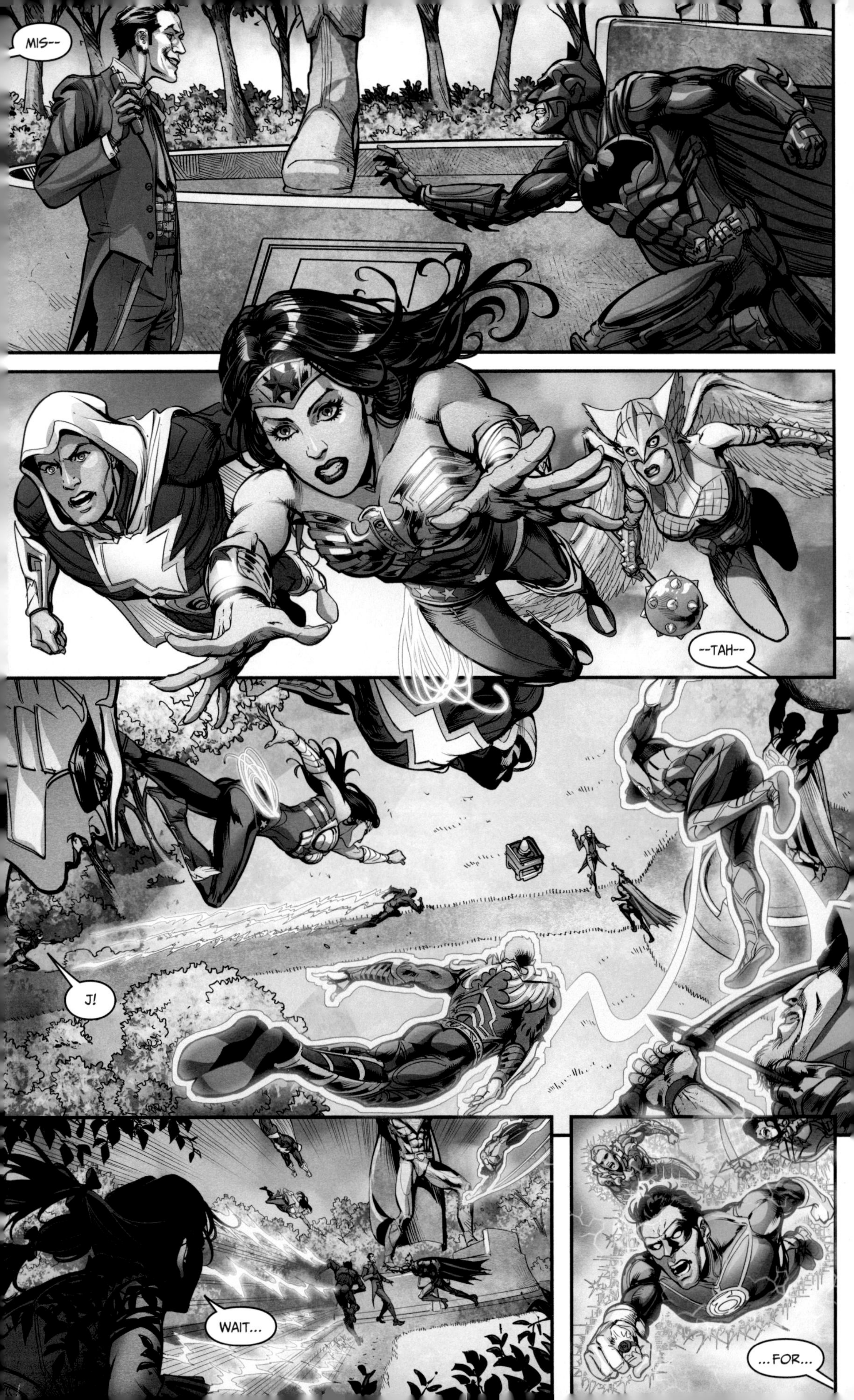
MIS--
--TAH--
J!
WAIT...
...FOR...

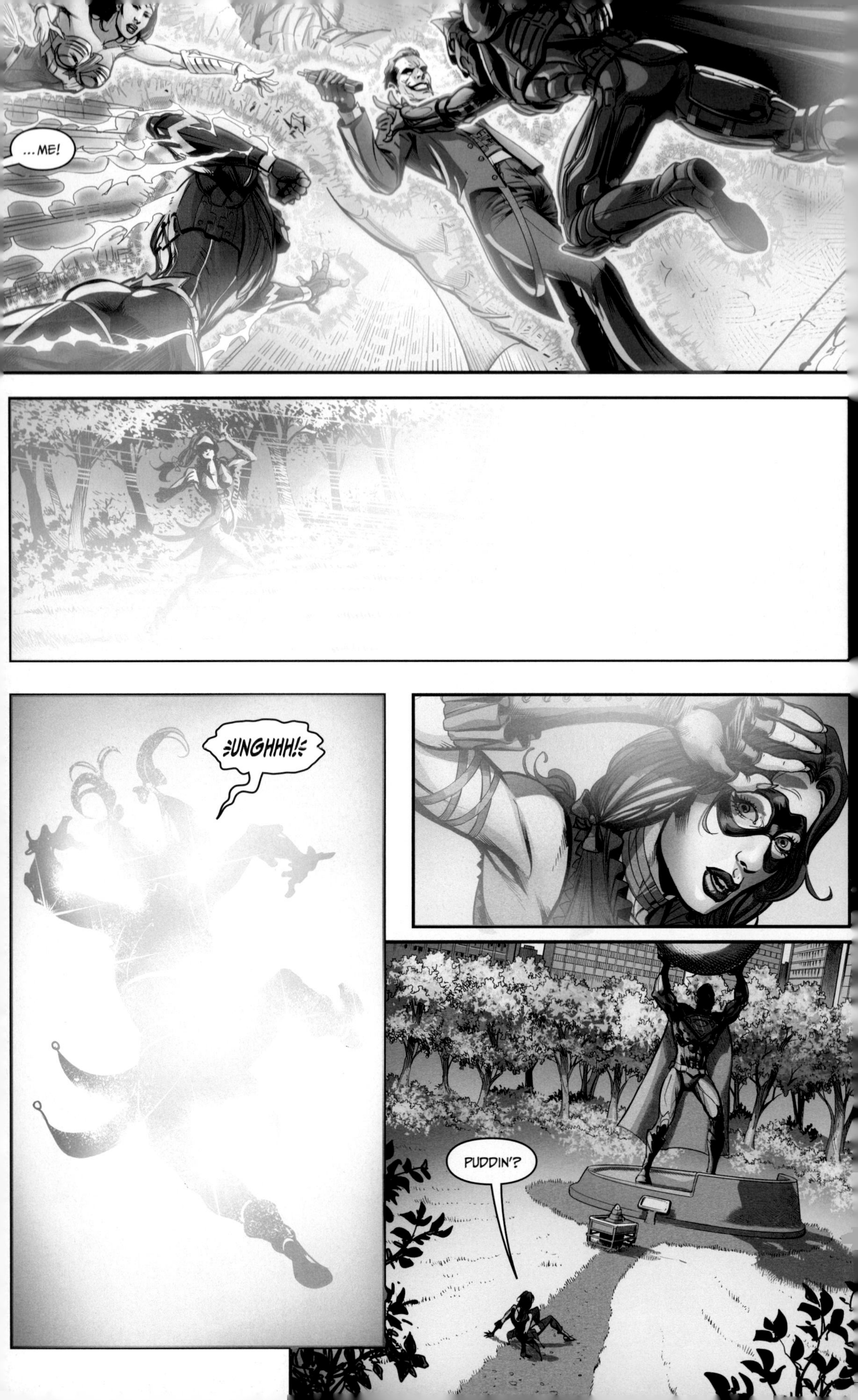
...ME!
UNGHHH!
PUDDIN'?

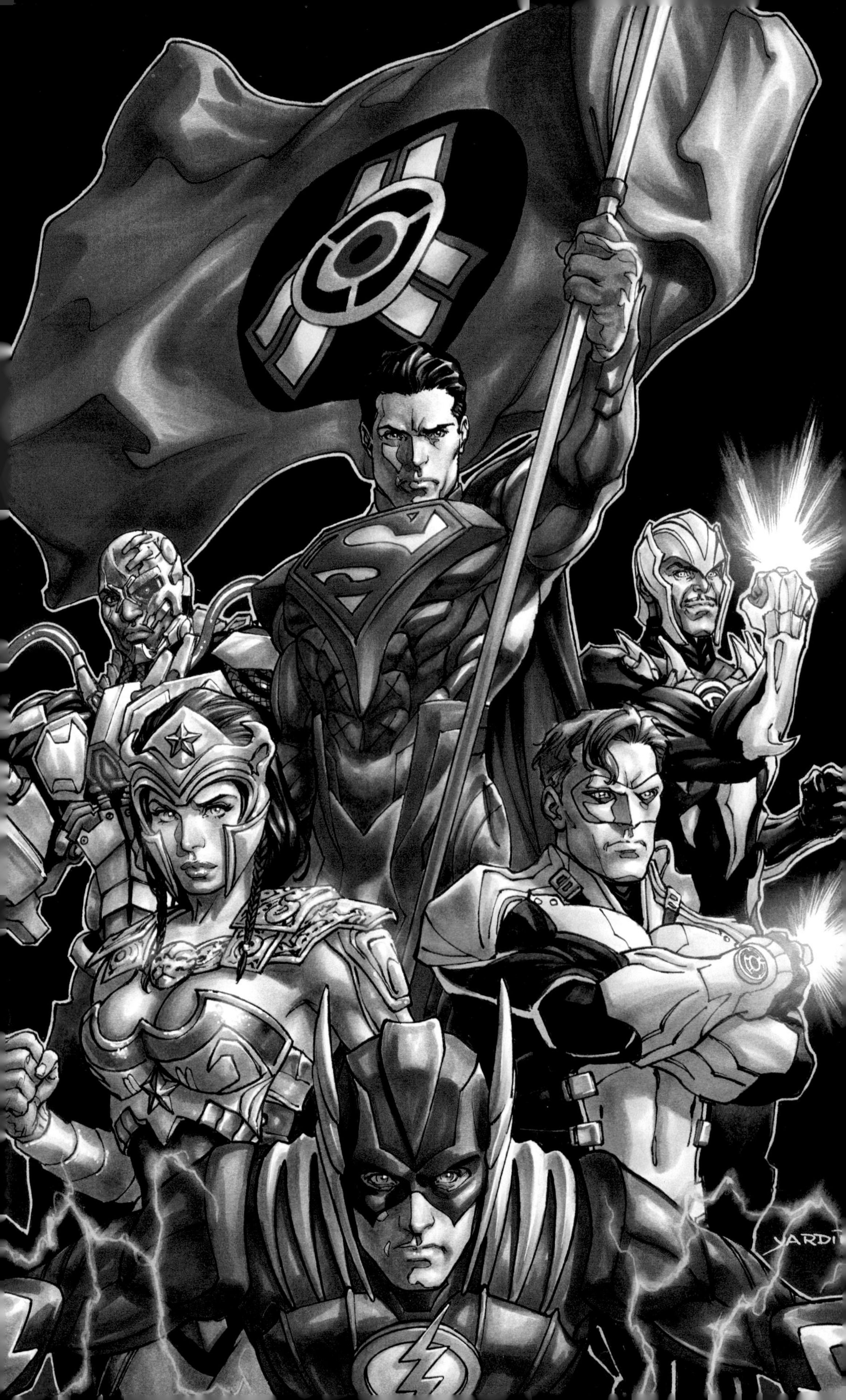

"The Final Gambit" **Mike S. Miller** Artist **J. Nanjan** Colorist

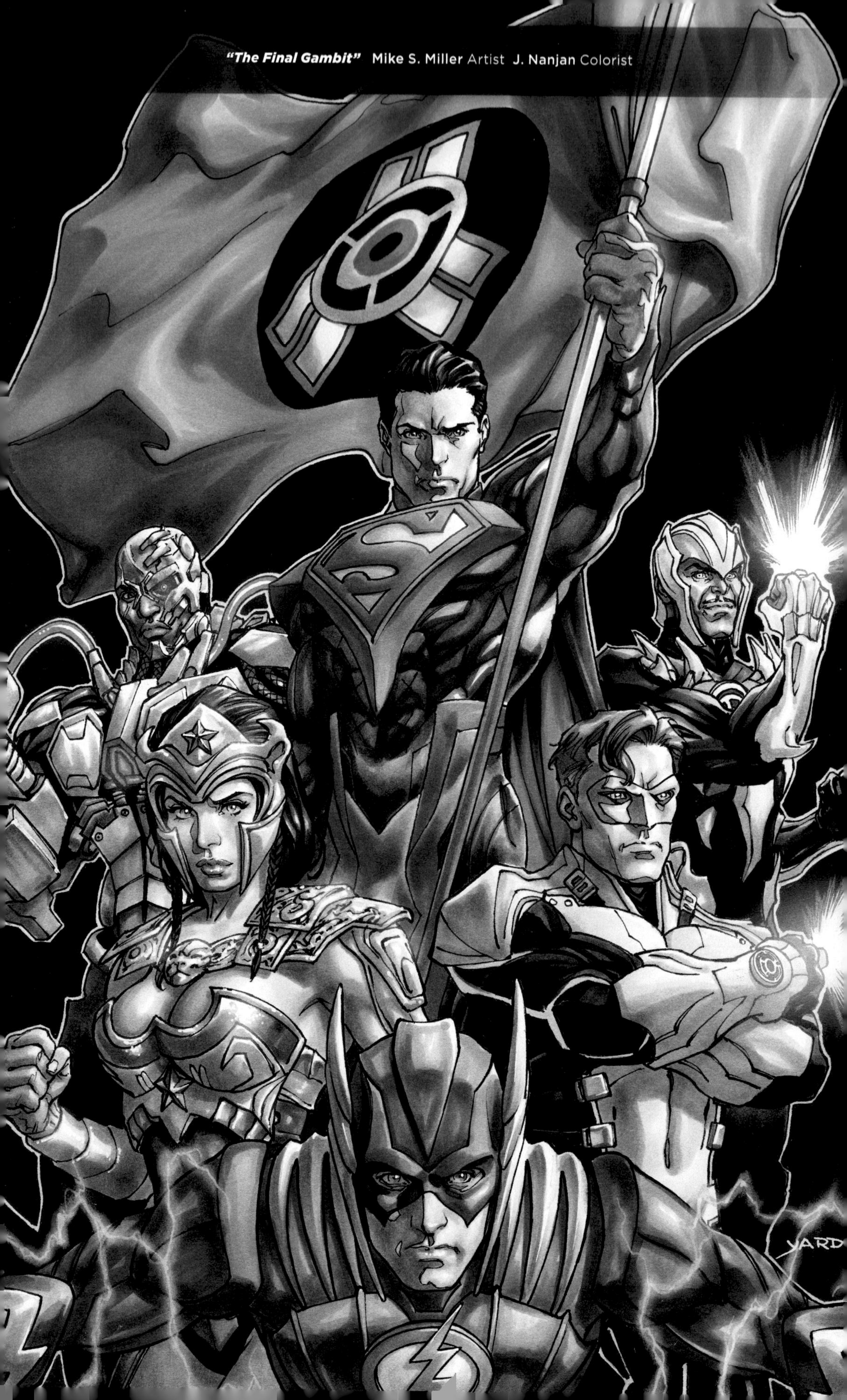
YARD

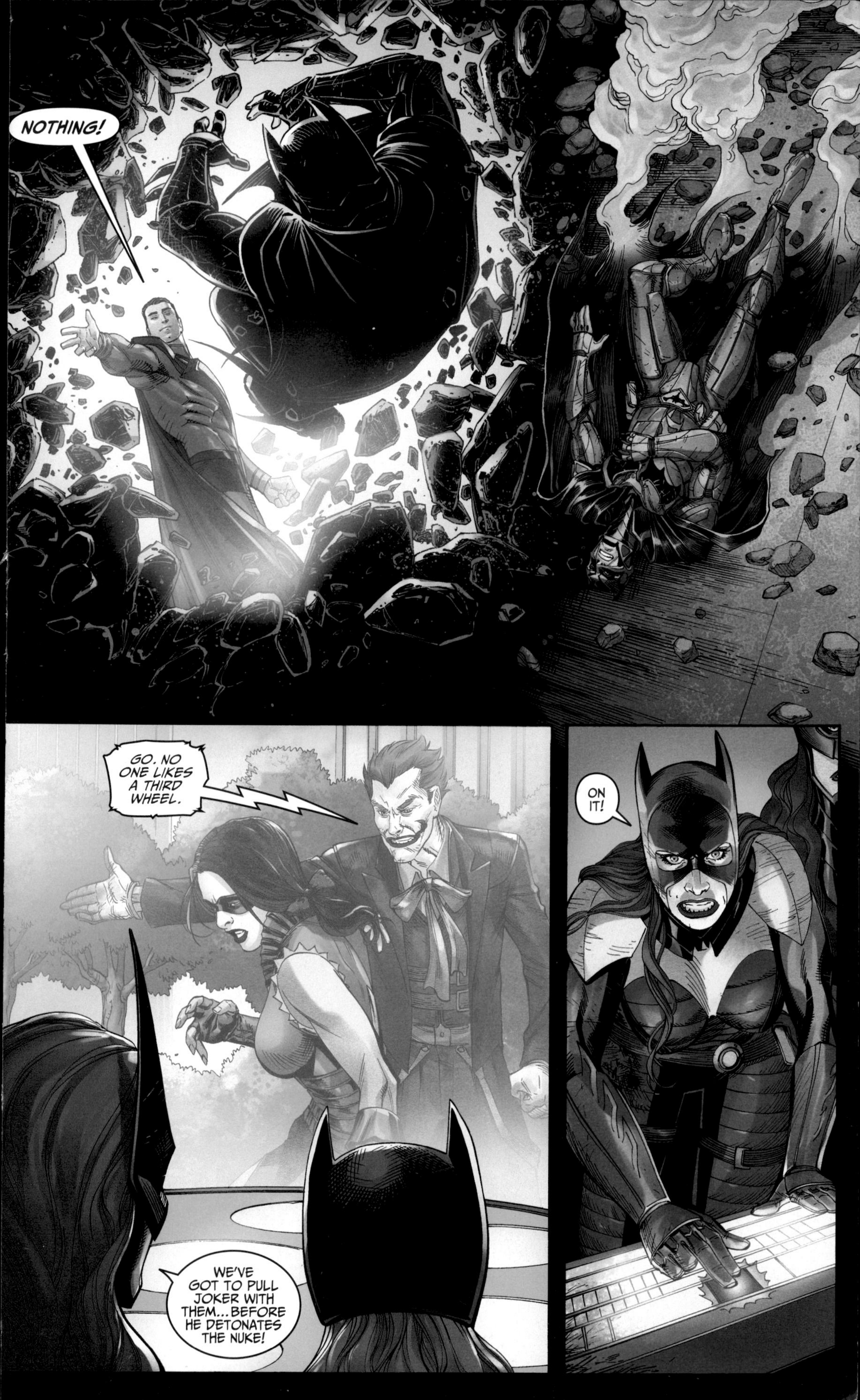
NOTHING!
GO. NO ONE LIKES A THIRD WHEEL.
WE'VE GOT TO PULL JOKER WITH THEM...BEFORE HE DETONATES THE NUKE!
ON IT!

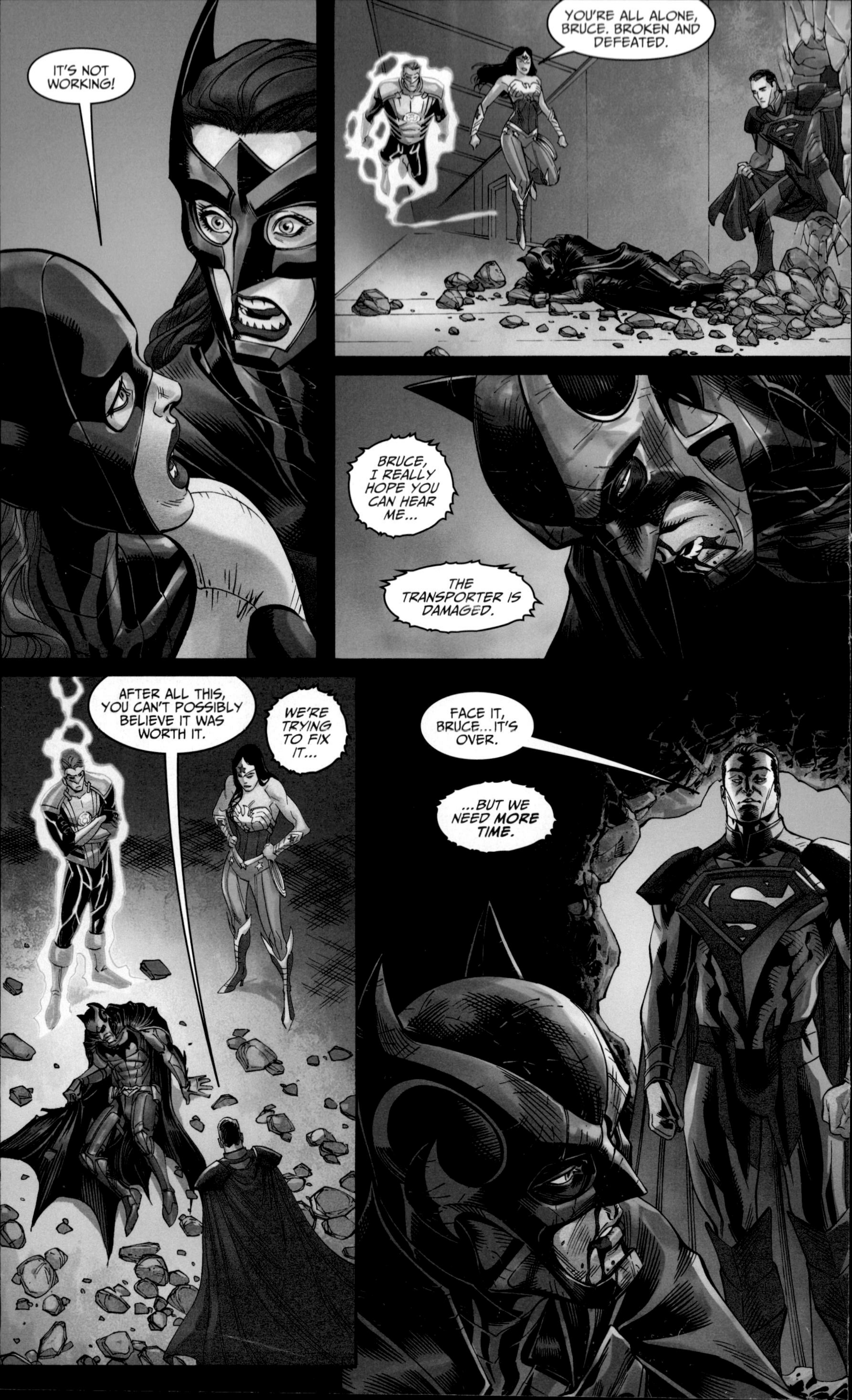
IT'S NOT WORKING!
YOU'RE ALL ALONE, BRUCE. BROKEN AND DEFEATED.
BRUCE, I REALLY HOPE YOU CAN HEAR ME...
THE TRANSPORTER IS DAMAGED.
AFTER ALL THIS, YOU CAN'T POSSIBLY BELIEVE IT WAS WORTH IT.
WE'RE TRYING TO FIX IT...
FACE IT, BRUCE...IT'S OVER.
...BUT WE NEED MORE TIME.

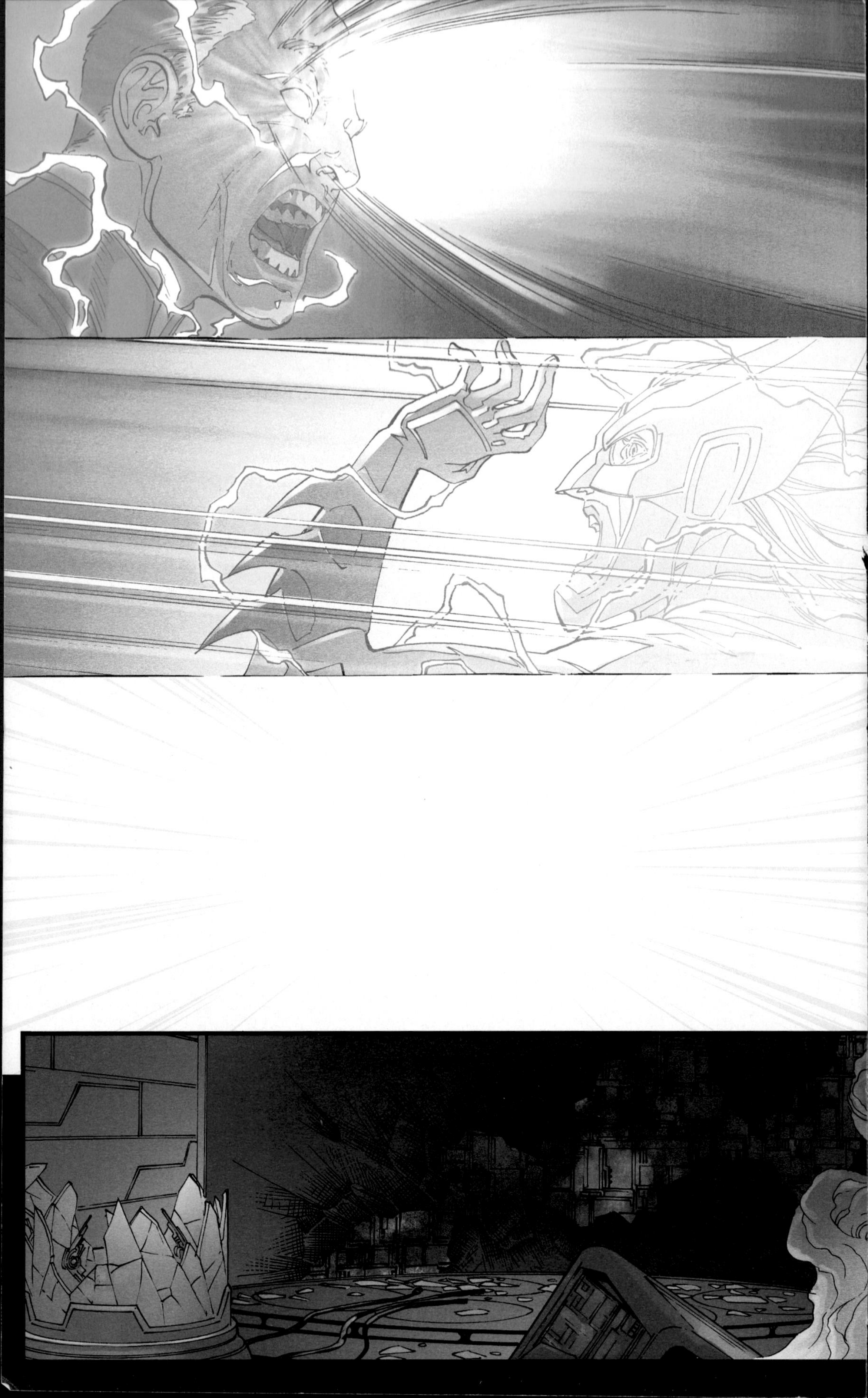

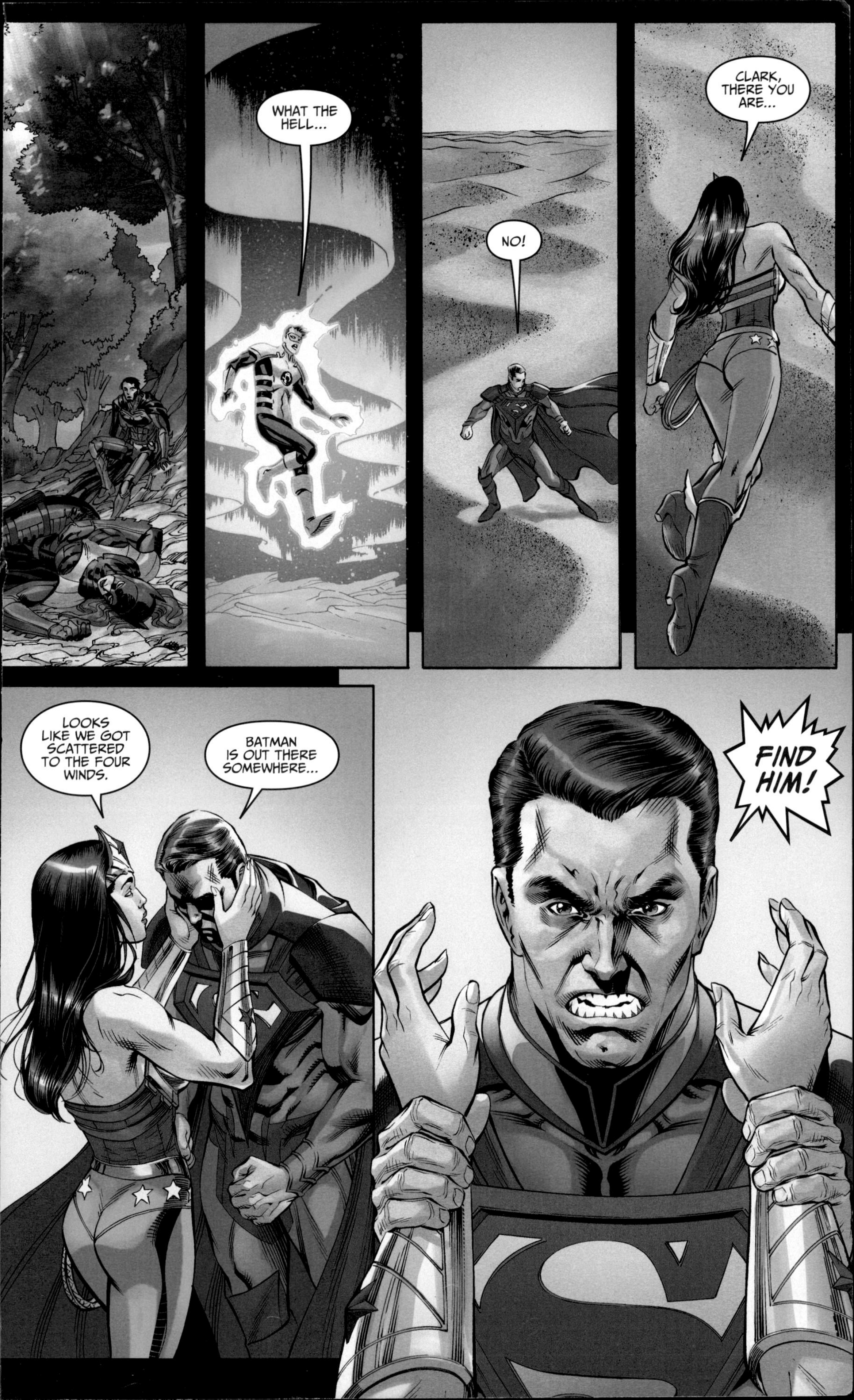
WHAT THE HELL...
NO!
CLARK, THERE YOU ARE...
LOOKS LIKE WE GOT SCATTERED TO THE FOUR WINDS.
BATMAN IS OUT THERE SOMEWHERE...
FIND HIM!